CONTENTS

Introduction

Stir-frying is quick, easy, healthy and an ideal way of producing delicious and nutritious meals. However, there is even more to the versatile wok than this; it can be used for steaming, braising and deep-frying, too. Designed to spread the heat quickly and evenly, it is truly a joy for any cook to use, and once you have acquired one, you will probably never want your saucepans and frying pans again!

∞

Wok cookery originated in China, and similar techniques are widespread throughout South-east Asia and India. Many traditional dishes from the cuisines of these countries have inspired the mouth-watering recipes in this book – from Balti curries to Chinese stir-fries and from spicy Thai vegetables to Indonesian rice dishes. Western cooks have been quick to recognize the ease and speed of wok cookery and so recipes that marry the best of east and west are also featured.

∞

The book includes a basic introduction to using a wok and a guide to some of the more exotic ingredients, as well as standard oriental sauces, spices and herbs. All the recipes are beautifully illustrated in colour with easy-to-follow step-by-step instructions. Hints and tips throughout the book advise on variations, best buys and ways of preparing some of the more unfamiliar ingredients.

∞

You will be surprised by the vast range of stir-fried foods and other delicious recipes that can be cooked in a wok. You will soon find yourself adapting your own favourites to this technique.

∞

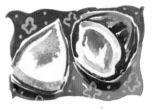

COOKING TECHNIQUES

STIR-FRYING

This quick technique retains the fresh flavour, colour and texture of ingredients and its success depends upon having all that you require ready prepared before starting to cook.

1 Heat an empty wok over a high heat. This prevents food sticking and will ensure an even heat. Add the oil and swirl it around so that it coats the base and halfway up the sides of the wok. It is important that the oil is hot when the food is added, so that it will start to cook immediately.

2 Add the ingredients in the order specified in the recipe: usually aromatics first (garlic, ginger, spring onions). If this is the case, do not wait for the oil to get so hot that it is almost smoking or they will burn and become bitter. Toss them in the oil for a few seconds. Next add the main ingredients that require longer cooking, such as dense vegetables or meat. Follow with the faster-cooking items. Toss the ingredients from the centre of the wok to the sides using a wok scoop, long-handled spoon or wooden spatula.

DEEP-FRYING

A wok is ideal for deep-frying as it uses far less oil than a deep-fat fryer. Make sure that it is fully secure on its stand before adding the oil and never leave the wok unattended.

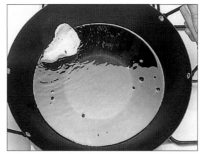

1 Put the wok on a stand and half fill with oil. Heat until the required temperature registers on a thermometer. Alternatively, test it by dropping in a small piece of food; if bubbles form all over the surface of the food, the oil is ready.

2 Carefully add the food to the oil, using long wooden chopsticks or tongs, and move it around to prevent it sticking together. Use a bamboo strainer or slotted spoon to remove the food. Drain on kitchen paper before serving.

STEAMING

Steamed foods are cooked by a gentle, moist heat which must circulate freely in order for the food to cook. Steaming is increasingly popular with health-conscious cooks as it preserves flavour and nutrients. It is perfect for vegetables, meat, poultry and especially fish. The easiest way to steam food in a wok is using a bamboo steamer.

USING A BAMBOO STEAMER

1 Put the wok on a stand. Pour in sufficient boiling water to come about 5cm/2in up the sides and bring back to simmering point. Carefully put the bamboo steamer into the wok so that it rests securely against the sloping sides without touching the surface of the water.

2 Cover the steamer with its matching lid and cook for the time recommended in the recipe. Check the water level from time to time and top up with boiling water if necessary.

USING A WOK AS A STEAMER

1 Put a trivet in the wok, then place the wok securely on its stand. Pour in sufficient boiling water to come just below the trivet. Carefully place a plate containing the food to be steamed on the trivet.

2 Cover the wok with its lid, bring the water back to the boil, then lower the heat so that it is simmering gently. Steam for the time recommended in the recipe. Check the water level from time to time and top up with boiling water if necessary.

Index

INGREDIENTS

BAMBOO SHOOTS
These mild-flavoured tender shoots of the young bamboo are widely available fresh or sliced or halved in cans.

BEANSPROUTS
These shoots of the mung bean are usually available from supermarkets. They add a crisp texture to stir-fries.

1 Pick over the beansprouts and discard any that are discoloured, broken or wilted.

2 Rinse the beansprouts under cold running water and drain well.

CHINESE FIVE-SPICE POWDER
This flavouring contains star anise, pepper, fennel, cloves and cinnamon.

CHINESE PANCAKES
These unseasoned, flour-and-water pancakes are available fresh or frozen.

CHINESE RICE WINE
It has a rich, sherry-like flavour and can be found in most large super-markets and oriental food stores. Sherry may be used as a substitute.

CREAMED COCONUT
This is available in a solid block from oriental food stores and large super-markets. It gives an intense coconut flavour; simply add water to make a thick coconut paste. It can be thinned with more water if required.

GINGER
Ginger has a sharp distinctive flavour. Choose firm, plump pieces of fresh root with unwrinkled, shiny skins.

1 Using a small sharp knife, peel the skin from the root.

2 Place the ginger on a board. Set the flat side of a cleaver or chef's knife on top and strike it firmly with your fist to soften its fibrous texture.

3 Chop the ginger as coarsely or finely as you wish, moving the blade backwards and forwards.

GRAM FLOUR
Made from ground chick-peas, this flour has a unique flavour and is worth seeking out in Indian food stores.

KAFFIR LIME LEAVES
These are used rather like bay leaves, but to give an aromatic lime flavour to dishes. The fresh leaves are available from oriental food stores and can be frozen for future use.

1 Using a small sharp knife, remove the centre vein.

2 Cut the leaves crossways into very fine strips.

LEMON GRASS
This herb imparts a mild, sour-sweet, citrus flavour. Split and use whole, finely chopped or ground to a paste.

MOOLI
Mooli is a member of the radish family with a fresh, slightly peppery taste. Unlike other radishes, it is good when cooked, but should be salted and allowed to drain first, as it has a high water content. It is widely used in Chinese cooking and may be carved into an elaborate garnish.

OKRA
This edible seed pod is a member of the hibiscus family and is also known as bhindi, gumbo and ladies' fingers. It is widely used in Indian cuisine.

OYSTER SAUCE
Made from oyster extract, it is used in many fish dishes, soups and sauces.

PLUM SAUCE
This is a sweet and sour sauce with a unique fruity flavour.

RED BEAN PASTE
This reddish-brown paste is made from puréed red beans and crystallized sugar. It is usually sold in cans.

RICE
Long grain rice is generally used for savoury dishes. There are many high-quality varieties, coming from a range of countries. Basmati, which means fragrant in Hindi, is generally acknowledged as the prince or king of rices and is probably the ideal choice for Balti recipes that suggest serving the dish with it. Thai jasmine rice is also fragrant and slightly sticky.

RICE WINE
Made from glutinous rice, Chinese rice wine is also known as yellow wine – *Huang Jiu* or *Chiew* – because of its colour. The best variety is called *Shao Hsing* or *Shaoxing* and comes from the south-east of China. Dry or medium sherry may be used as substitute.

SALTED BLACK BEANS
Sold in plastic bags and jars, these very

Toffee Apples

A variety of fruits, such as bananas and pineapple, can be prepared and cooked in this way.

INGREDIENTS

Serves 4
4 firm eating apples
115g/4oz plain flour
about 120ml/4fl oz/½ cup water
1 egg, beaten
vegetable oil, for deep-frying, plus
   30ml/2 tbsp for the toffee
115g/4oz sugar

1 Peel and core each apple and cut into eight pieces. Dust each piece of apple with a little of the flour.

2 Sift the remaining flour into a mixing bowl, then slowly add the cold water and stir well to make a smooth batter. Add the beaten egg and blend well.

3 Heat the oil for deep-frying in a wok. Dip the apple pieces in the batter and deep-fry for about 3 minutes or until golden. Remove and drain. Drain off the oil.

4 Heat the remaining oil in the wok, add the sugar and stir continuously until the sugar has caramelized. Quickly add the apple pieces and blend well so that each piece of apple is thoroughly coated with the toffee. Dip the apple pieces in cold water to harden before serving.

salty and pungent beans should be crushed with water or wine before use. They will keep almost indefinitely in a screw-top jar.

SESAME OIL
This is used more for flavouring than for cooking. It is very intensely flavoured, so only a little is required.

SHALLOTS
Mild-flavoured members of the onion family, shallots are used in many flavourings and sauces, such as Thai curry paste. Fried in crisp flakes, they can be used as a garnish.

SOY SAUCE
Made from the naturally fermented soy bean, this is an important ingredient in most oriental cooking.

SPRING ONIONS
These are widely used in stir-fried dishes, The thinner the onion, the milder it will be. Chop off the roots and the top part of the green section,

---

COOK'S TIP

Coconut milk is an important ingredient in Thai, Indonesian and other South-east Asian cuisines. It is not the same as the "milk" found inside the coconut naturally, but is made from the unsweetened, grated flesh mixed with water. It is available in cans, compressed blocks or in powder form.

To make your own, break open a fresh coconut and remove the brown inner skin from the flesh. Grate sufficient flesh to measure 400ml/14 fl oz/1⅔ cups. Place the grated flesh, together with 300ml/½ pint/1¼ cups water, in a blender or food processor fitted with a metal blade and process for 1 minute. Strain the mixture through a sieve lined with muslin into a bowl. Gather up the corners of the muslin and squeeze out the liquid. The coconut milk is then ready to use, but you should stir before use.

---

then chop finely or cut into matchstick strips. In some recipes, the green and white parts are kept separate for an extra decorative effect.

SPRING ROLL WRAPPERS
Paper-thin wrappers made from wheat or rice flour and water, they are available from oriental food stores. Wheat wrappers are usually sold frozen and should be thawed and separated before use. Rice flour wrappers are dry and must be soaked before use.

SZECHUAN PEPPERCORNS
Also known as *farchiew*, these aromatic, red peppercorns are best used roasted and ground. They are not so hot as either white or black peppercorns, but do add a unique taste to food.

TAMARIND
This is the brown sticky pulp of the bean-like seed pod of the tamarind tree. It is used in Thai and Indonesian cooking to add tartness to recipes, rather like western cooks use vinegar or lemon juice. It is usually sold dried or pulped. The pulp is diluted with water and strained before use. Soak 25g/1oz tamarind pulp in 150ml/¼ pint/⅔ cup warm water for about 10 minutes. Squeeze out as much tamarind juice as possible by pressing all the liquid through a sieve.

THAI CURRY PASTES
Curry paste is traditionally made by pounding fresh herbs and spices in a mortar with a pestle. There are two types – red and green – made with red and green chillies respectively. Other ingredients vary with individual cooks, but red curry paste typically contains ginger, shallots, garlic, coriander and cumin seeds and lime juice, as well as chillies. Herbs and flavourings in green curry paste usually include spring onions, fresh coriander, kaffir lime leaves, ginger, garlic and lemon grass. Making curry paste is time-consuming, but it tastes excellent and keeps well.

Ready-made pastes, available in packets and tubs, are satisfactory substitutes.

THAI FISH SAUCE
This is used in Thai recipes in much the same way as soy sauce is used in Chinese recipes.

TOFU
Also known as bean curd, tofu is bland in flavour but readily absorbs the flavours of the food with which it is cooked. Firm blocks of tofu are best suited to stir-frying. Store, covered with water, in the refrigerator.

TURMERIC
A member of the ginger family, turmeric is a rich, golden-coloured root. If you are using the fresh root, wear rubber gloves when peeling it to avoid staining your skin.

WATER CHESTNUTS
This walnut-sized bulb comes from an Asian water plant and looks like a sweet chestnut. They are sold fresh by some oriental food stores, but are more readily available canned.

WONTON WRAPPERS
These paper-thin squares of yellow-coloured dough are available from most oriental food stores.

WILD RICE
This is not, in fact, rice at all, but a form of aquatic grass. While not a traditional, oriental "rice", it has now become very popular. It takes a long time to cook – up to 50 minutes – and is often sold in combination with long grain and basmati rice.

YELLOW BEAN SAUCE
This thick paste is made from salted, fermented yellow soy beans, crushed with flour and sugar.

Sopaipillas

INGREDIENTS

Makes about 30
225g/8oz plain flour, sifted
15ml/1 tbsp baking powder
5ml/1 tsp salt
30ml/2 tbsp lard or margarine
175ml/6fl oz/³/₄ cup water
corn oil, for deep-frying
syrup or honey, to serve

COOK'S TIP

Use your imagination when deciding what to serve with the puffs. Sprinkle them with cinnamon and sugar, or flavour syrup with rum. The fat little pillows could even be served plain, as they taste delicious.

1 Put the flour, baking powder and salt into a large bowl. Lightly rub in the lard or margarine, using your fingertips, until the mixture resembles coarse breadcrumbs.

2 Gradually stir in the water, using a fork, until the mixture clumps together to form a soft dough.

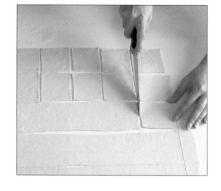

3 Shape the dough into a ball, then turn out on to a lightly floured surface and knead very gently until smooth. Roll out thinly to a rectangle measuring about 46 x 35cm/l8 x l4in. Using a sharp knife, carefully cut into about 30 7.5cm/3in squares. For a decorative edge, you could use a pastry wheel to cut out the squares.

4 Heat the oil to 190°C/375°F or until a cube of day-old bread browns in 30–60 seconds.

5 Fry the puffs, a few at a time, in the oil. As they puff up, turn over to cook the other side. Remove with a slotted spoon and drain on kitchen paper. Serve with syrup or honey.

SOUPS AND STARTERS

Delicately flavoured soups, crisp deep-fried spring rolls, spicy seafood and gloriously self-indulgent ribs and wings are only some of the deliciously different starters that can be easily and quickly prepared in a wok. Wok and stir-fry cooking can be used to full advantage for the first course when entertaining, as you can prepare all the ingredients in advance, which means you can spend time with your guests and still produce a mouth-watering start to the meal – apparently without any effort and in a matter of mere moments.

Buñuelos

INGREDIENTS

Serves 6

225g/8oz/2 cups plain flour
5ml/1 tsp baking powder
2.5ml/½ tsp salt
15ml/1 tbsp granulated sugar
1 large egg, beaten
120ml/4fl oz/½ cup milk
25g/1oz/2 tbsp unsalted butter, melted
oil, for frying
sugar, for dusting

For the syrup

225g/8oz/1⅓ cups soft light
  brown sugar
750ml/1¼ pints/3 cups water
2.5cm/1in cinnamon stick
1 clove

1 Make the syrup. Combine all the ingredients in a saucepan. Heat, stirring, until the sugar has dissolved, then simmer until the mixture is reduced to a light syrup. Remove and discard the spices. Keep the syrup warm while you make the *buñuelos*.

2 Sift the flour, baking powder and salt into a bowl. Stir in the sugar. In a mixing bowl, whisk the egg and the milk well together. Gradually stir in the dry mixture, then beat in the melted butter to make a soft dough.

3 Turn the dough on to a lightly floured board and knead until it is smooth and elastic. Divide the dough into 18 even-size pieces. Shape into balls. With your hands, flatten the balls to disk shapes about 2cm/¾in thick.

4 Use the floured handle of a wooden spoon to poke a hole through the centre of each *buñuelo*. Pour oil into a deep-frying pan to a depth of 5cm/2in. Alternatively, use a deep-fryer. Heat the oil to a termperature of 190°C/375°F, or until a cube of day-old bread added to the oil browns in 30–60 seconds.

5 Fry the fritters in batches, taking care not to overcrowd the pan, until they are puffy and golden brown on both sides. Lift out with a slotted spoon and drain on kitchen paper.

6 Dust the *buñuelos* with sugar and serve with the syrup.

--- COOK'S TIP ---

Make the syrup ahead of time if you prefer, and chill it until ready to use, when it can be warmed through quickly.

Sweetcorn and Chicken Soup

This popular classic Chinese soup is delicious and extremely easy to make in a wok.

INGREDIENTS

Serves 4-6

1 chicken breast fillet, about 115g/
    4oz, skinned and cubed
10ml/2 tsp light soy sauce
15ml/1 tbsp Chinese rice wine or
    dry sherry
5ml/1 tsp cornflour
60ml/4 tbsp cold water
5ml/ 1 tsp sesame oil
30ml/2 tbsp groundnut oil
5ml/1 tsp grated fresh root ginger
1 litre/1¾ pints/4 cups chicken stock
425g/15oz can creamed sweetcorn
225g/8oz can sweetcorn kernels
2 eggs, beaten
salt and ground black pepper
2–3 spring onions, green parts only,
    cut into tiny rounds, to garnish

1 Mince the chicken in a food processor or blender, taking care not to over-process. Transfer the chicken to a bowl and stir in the soy sauce, rice wine or sherry, cornflour, water, sesame oil and seasoning. Cover and leave for about 15 minutes to absorb the flavours.

2 Heat a wok over a medium heat. Add the groundnut oil and swirl it around. Add the ginger and stir-fry for a few seconds. Add the stock, creamed sweetcorn and sweetcorn kernels. Bring to just below boiling point.

3 Spoon about 90ml/6 tbsp of the hot liquid into the chicken mixture and stir until it forms a smooth paste. Add to the wok. Slowly bring to the boil, stirring constantly, then simmer for 2–3 minutes until cooked.

4 Pour the beaten eggs into the soup in a slow, steady stream, using a fork or chopsticks to stir the top of the soup in a figure-of-eight pattern. The egg should set in lacy threads. Serve immediately with the spring onions sprinkled over.

Fried Bananas

These delicious treats are a favourite among children and adults alike. They are sold as snacks all day and night at portable roadside stalls and market places throughout Thailand. This recipe works just as well with other fruits, such as pineapple and apple.

INGREDIENTS

Serves 4
115g/4oz plain flour
2.5ml/½ tsp bicarbonate of soda
30ml/2 tbsp sugar
1 egg
90ml/6 tbsp water
30ml/2 tbsp shredded coconut or
   15ml/1tbsp sesame seeds
4 firm bananas
oil for deep-frying
salt
30ml/2 tbsp clear honey, to serve
mint sprigs and lychees, to decorate

1 Sift the flour, bicarbonate of soda and a pinch of salt into a bowl. Stir in the sugar. Whisk in the egg and just enough water to make a thin batter. Then whisk in the shredded coconut or the sesame seeds.

2 Peel the bananas. Carefully cut each one in half lengthways, then cut in half crossways.

3 Heat the oil in a preheated wok. Dip the bananas in the batter, then gently drop a few pieces at a time into the hot oil. Fry until golden brown.

4 Remove the bananas from the oil and drain on kitchen paper. Serve immediately with honey, if using, and decorate with mint sprigs and lychees.

--- COOK'S TIP ---

Buy bananas that are just approaching ripeness and are mostly yellow but still green at the tips so that they hold their shape and do not disintegrate during cooking. Completely ripe bananas – with yellow, speckled skins – are likely to fall apart, but will be very sweet.

Chicken and Asparagus Soup

This is a very delicate and delicious soup, with chicken and asparagus simply and quickly prepared in a wok.

INGREDIENTS

Serves 4
150g/5oz chicken breast fillet
5ml/1 tsp egg white
5ml/1 tsp cornflour paste
115g/4oz fresh or canned asparagus
750ml/1¼ pints/3 cups stock
salt and ground black pepper
fresh coriander leaves, to garnish

1 Cut the chicken meat into thin slices, each about the size of a postage stamp. Mix with a pinch of salt, then add the egg white and finally the cornflour paste.

2 Discard the tough stems of the asparagus, and cut the tender spears diagonally into short lengths.

3 Bring the stock to a rolling boil in a wok. Add the asparagus, bring back to the boil and cook for 2 minutes. (This is not necessary if you are using canned asparagus.)

4 Add the chicken, stir to separate and bring back to the boil once more. Adjust the seasoning to taste. Serve hot, garnished with fresh coriander leaves.

Mango and Coconut Stir-fry

Choose a ripe mango for this recipe. If you buy one that is a little under-ripe, leave it in a warm place for a day or two before using.

INGREDIENTS

Serves 4
¼ coconut
1 large, ripe mango
juice of 2 limes
rind of 2 limes, finely grated
15ml/1 tbsp sunflower oil
15g/½ oz butter
30ml/2 tbsp clear honey
crème fraîche, to serve

1 Prepare the coconut by draining the milk and peeling the flesh with a vegetable peeler.

2 Peel the mango. Cut the stone out of the middle of the fruit. Cut each half of the mango into slices.

3 Place the mango slices in a bowl and pour over the lime juice and rind, to marinate them.

4 Meanwhile heat a wok, then add 10ml/2 tsp of the oil. When the oil is hot, add the butter. When the butter has melted, stir in the coconut flakes and stir-fry for 1–2 minutes until the coconut is golden brown. Remove and drain on kitchen paper. Wipe out the wok. Strain the mango slices, reserving the juice.

5 Heat the wok and add the remaining oil. When the oil is hot, add the mango and stir-fry for 1–2 minutes, then add the juice and allow to bubble and reduce for 1 minute. Stir in the honey, sprinkle on the coconut flakes and serve with crème fraîche.

Corn and Crab Meat Soup

Surprisingly, this soup originated in the United States, but it has since been introduced into mainstream Chinese cookery. It is important that you make sure you use creamed sweetcorn in the recipe to achieve exactly the right consistency.

INGREDIENTS

Serves 4

115g/4oz crab meat or chicken
    breast fillet
2.5ml/½ tsp finely chopped root ginger
2 egg whites
30ml/2 tbsp milk
15ml/1 tbsp cornflour paste
600ml/1 pint/2½ cups stock
225g/8oz can creamed sweetcorn
salt and ground black pepper
finely chopped spring onions,
    to garnish

1 Flake the crab meat roughly with chopsticks or chop the chicken breast. Mix the crab meat or chicken with the chopped root ginger.

2 Beat the egg whites until frothy, add the milk and cornflour paste and beat again until smooth. Blend with the crab meat or chicken breast.

3 Bring the stock to the boil in a wok. Add the creamed sweetcorn and bring back to the boil once more.

4 Stir in the crab meat or chicken breast and egg-white mixture, adjust the seasoning and simmer gently until cooked. Serve garnished with finely chopped spring onions.

Classic Noodle Pudding

A traditional Jewish recipe, Classic Noodle Pudding is a rich and comforting dessert. It is also quite delicious.

INGREDIENTS

Serves 4–6

175g/6oz wide egg noodles
225g/8oz cottage cheese
115g/4oz cream cheese
75g/3oz caster sugar
2 eggs
120ml/4fl oz/½ cup soured cream
5ml/1 tsp vanilla essence
pinch of ground cinnamon
pinch of grated nutmeg
2.5ml/½ tsp grated lemon rind
50g/2oz butter
25g/1oz nibbed almonds
25g/1oz fine dried white breadcrumbs
icing sugar for dusting

1 Preheat the oven to 180°C/350°F/ Gas 4. Grease a shallow baking dish. Cook the noodles in a large saucepan of boiling water until just tender. Drain well.

2 Beat the cottage cheese, cream cheese and sugar together in a bowl. Add the eggs, one at a time, and stir in the soured cream. Stir in the vanilla essence, cinnamon, nutmeg and lemon rind.

3 Fold the noodles into the cheese mixture. Spoon into the prepared baking dish and level the surface.

4 Melt the butter in a frying pan. Add the almonds and fry for about 1 minute. Remove from the heat.

5 Stir in the breadcrumbs, mixing well. Sprinkle the mixture over the pudding. Bake for 30–40 minutes or until the mixture is set. Serve hot, dusted with a little icing sugar.

Hot and Sour Soup

This must surely be the best-known and all-time favourite soup in Chinese restaurants and take-aways throughout the world. It is fairly simple to make once you have got all the necessary ingredients together.

INGREDIENTS

Serves 4

4–6 dried Chinese mushrooms, soaked
   in warm water
115g/4oz pork or chicken
1 packet tofu
50g/2oz sliced bamboo shoots, drained
600ml/1pint/2½ cups stock
15ml/1 tbsp Chinese rice wine or
   dry sherry
15ml/1 tbsp light soy sauce
15ml/1 tbsp rice vinegar
salt and ground white pepper
15ml/1 tbsp cornflour paste

1 Squeeze the soaked mushrooms dry, then discard the hard stalks. Thinly shred the mushrooms, meat, tofu and bamboo shoots.

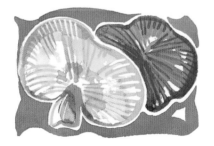

2 Bring the stock to a rolling boil in a wok and add the shredded ingredients. Bring back to the boil and simmer for about 1 minute.

3 Add the wine or sherry, soy sauce and vinegar and season. Bring back to the boil, then add the cornflour paste, stir until thickened and serve.

Pancakes Filled with Sweet Coconut

Traditionally, the pale green colour in the batter for *Dadar Gulung* was obtained from the juice squeezed from *pandan* leaves – a real labour of love. Green food colouring can be used as the modern alternative to this lengthy process.

INGREDIENTS

Makes 12–15 pancakes

175g/6oz dark brown sugar
450ml/15fl oz/scant 2 cups water
1 *pandan* leaf, stripped through with a fork and tied into a knot
175g/6oz desiccated coconut
oil for frying
salt

For the pancake batter

225g/8oz plain flour, sifted
2 eggs, beaten
2 drops of edible green food colouring
few drops of vanilla essence
450ml/15fl oz/scant 2 cups water
45ml/3 tbsp groundnut oil

1 Dissolve the sugar in the water with the *pandan* leaf, in a pan over gentle heat, stirring all the time. Increase the heat and allow to boil gently for 3–4 minutes, until the mixture just becomes syrupy. Do not let it caramelize.

2 Put the coconut into a wok with a pinch of salt. Pour over the prepared sugar syrup and cook over a very gentle heat, stirring from time to time, until the mixture becomes almost dry; this will take 5–10 minutes. Set aside until required.

3 To make the batter, blend together the flour, eggs, food colouring, vanilla essence, water and oil either by hand or in a food processor.

4 Brush an 18cm/7in frying pan with oil and cook 12–15 pancakes. Keep the pancakes warm. Fill each pancake with a generous spoonful of the coconut mixture, roll up and serve them immediately.

Wonton Soup

In China, wonton soup is served as a snack or dim sum rather than as a soup course during a large meal.

INGREDIENTS

Serves 4
175g/6oz pork, not too lean,
  roughly chopped
50g/2oz peeled prawns, finely minced
5ml/1 tsp light brown sugar
15ml/1 tbsp Chinese rice wine or
  dry sherry
15ml/1 tbsp light soy sauce
5ml/1 tsp finely chopped spring onions
5ml/1 tsp finely chopped root ginger
24 ready-made wonton skins
about 750ml/1¼ pints/3 cups stock
15ml/1 tbsp light soy sauce
finely chopped spring onions,
  to garnish

1 In a bowl, mix the chopped pork and minced prawns with the sugar, rice wine or sherry, soy sauce, spring onions and chopped ginger root. Blend well and set aside for 25–30 minutes for the flavours to blend.

2 Place about 5ml/1 tsp of the filling at the centre of each wonton skin.

3 Wet the edges of each wonton with a little water and press them together with your fingers to seal, then fold each wonton over.

4 To cook, bring the stock to a rolling boil in a wok, add the wontons and cook for 4–5 minutes. Transfer to individual soup bowls, season with the soy sauce and garnish with the spring onions. Serve.

DESSERTS

*No meal is truly complete without something sweet – and preferably self-indulgent –
at the end. Stir-frying fruit helps to maintain its colour and shape, so cooking in a wok
is an excellent way to prepare tasty desserts to round off a meal in style. Other unusual
but easy-to-cook, delicious sweet dishes in this chapter include mouth-watering deep-fried
buñuelos (a kind of Mexican doughnut), a scrumptious Jewish noodle pudding, and
gloriously sticky Chinese toffee apples.*

Fried Wontons

These delicious vegetarian versions of the classic wontons are filled with bean curd, spring onions, garlic and ginger.

INGREDIENTS

Makes 30
30 wonton wrappers
1 egg, beaten
oil for deep-frying

For the filling
10ml/2 tsp vegetable oil
15ml/1 tbsp grated fresh root ginger
2 garlic cloves, finely chopped
225g/8oz firm bean curd
6 spring onions, finely chopped
10ml/2 tsp sesame oil
15ml/1 tbsp soy sauce
salt and freshly ground black pepper

For the dipping sauce
30ml/2 tbsp soy sauce
15ml/1 tbsp sesame oil
15ml/1 tbsp rice vinegar
2.5ml/½ tsp chilli oil
2.5ml/½ tsp honey
30ml/2 tbsp water

1 Line a large baking sheet with greaseproof paper or sprinkle lightly with flour, then set aside. To make the filling, heat the oil in a frying pan. Add the root ginger and garlic cloves and fry for 30 seconds. Crumble in the bean curd and stir-fry for a few minutes.

2 Add the spring onions, sesame oil and soy sauce to the pan. Stir well and taste for seasoning. Remove from the heat and set aside to cool.

3 Make the dipping sauce by combining all the ingredients in a bowl and mixing well.

4 Place a wonton wrapper on a board in a diamond position. Brush the edges lightly with beaten egg. Spoon 5ml/1 tsp of the filling on the centre of the wonton wrapper.

5 Pull the top corner down to the bottom corner, folding the wrapper over the filling to make a triangle. Press firmly to seal. Place on the prepared baking sheet. Repeat with the rest of the wonton wrappers.

6 Heat the oil in a deep-fryer or large saucepan. Carefully add the wontons, a few at a time, and cook for a few minutes until golden brown. Drain on kitchen paper, then serve at once with the dipping sauce.

Nutty Rice and Mushroom Stir-fry

This delicious and substantial supper dish can be eaten hot or cold with salads.

INGREDIENTS

Serves 4–6
350g/12oz long grain rice,
   preferably basmati
45ml/3 tbsp sunflower oil
1 small onion or shallot,
   roughly chopped
225g/8oz field mushrooms, sliced
50g/2oz hazelnuts, roughly chopped
50g/2oz pecan nuts, roughly
   chopped
50g/2oz almonds, roughly chopped
60ml/4 tbsp fresh parsley, chopped
salt and ground black pepper

1 Rinse the rice, then cook for 10–12 minutes in 700–900ml/ 1¼ –1½ pints/3–3¾ cups salted water in a saucepan with a tight-fitting lid. When cooked, refresh under cold water. Heat the wok, then add half the oil. Stir-fry the rice for 2–3 minutes. Remove and set aside.

--- COOK'S TIP ---

Of all the types of long grain rice, basmati is undoubtedly the king. This long, thin, aromatic grain grows in India, where its name means fragrant. Basmati rice benefits from rinsing in a bowl with plenty of cold water and a light soaking for 10 minutes.

2 Add the remaining oil and stir-fry the onion or shallot for 2 minutes until softened but not coloured. Mix in the field mushrooms and stir-fry for 2 minutes.

3 Add all the nuts and stir-fry for 1 minute. Return the rice to the wok and stir-fry for 3 minutes. Season with salt and pepper. Stir in the parsley and serve immediately.

Pork Dumplings

These dumplings, when shallow fried, make a good starter to a multi-course meal. They can also be steamed and served as a snack or poached in large quantities for a complete meal.

INGREDIENTS

Makes about 80–90
450g/1lb plain flour
about 475ml/16fl oz/2 cups water
flour, for dusting
salt

For the filling
450g/1lb Chinese leaves or
   white cabbage
450g/1lb minced pork
15ml/1 tbsp finely chopped
   spring onions
5ml/1 tsp finely chopped fresh
   root ginger
10ml/2 tsp salt
5ml/1 tsp light brown sugar
30ml/2 tbsp light soy sauce
15ml/1 tbsp Chinese rice wine or
   dry sherry
10ml/2 tsp sesame oil

For the dipping sauce
30ml/2 tbsp red chilli oil
15ml/1 tbsp light soy sauce
15ml/1 tbsp finely chopped garlic
15ml/1 tbsp finely chopped
   spring onions

1 Sift the flour into a bowl, then pour in the water and mix to a firm dough. Knead until smooth on a lightly floured surface, then cover with a damp cloth and set aside for 25–30 minutes.

2 For the filling, blanch the Chinese leaves or cabbage until soft. Drain and chop finely. Mix the cabbage with the pork, spring onions, ginger, salt, sugar, soy sauce, wine and sesame oil.

3 Lightly dust a work surface with the flour. Knead and roll the dough into a long sausage about 2.5cm/1in in diameter. Cut the sausage in about 80–90 small pieces and flatten each piece with the palm of your hand.

4 Using a rolling pin, roll out each piece into a thin pancake about 6cm/2½in in diameter.

5 Place about 25ml/1½ tbsp of the filling in the centre of each pancake and fold into a half-moon pouch. Pinch the edges firmly so that the dumpling is tightly sealed.

6 Bring 150ml/¼ pint/⅔ cup salted water to the boil in a wok. Add the dumplings and poach for 2 minutes. Remove the wok from the heat and leave the dumplings in the water for a further 15 minutes.

7 Make the dipping sauce by combining all the sauce ingredients in a bowl and mixing well. Serve in a small bowl with the dumplings.

Fried Rice with Spices

This dish is mildly spiced, suitable as an accompaniment to any curried dish. The whole spices – cloves, cardamom, bay leaf, cinnamon, peppercorns and cumin – are not intended to be eaten.

INGREDIENTS

Serves 3–4

175g/6oz basmati rice
2.5ml/¹⁄₂ tsp salt
15ml/1 tbsp ghee or butter
8 whole cloves
4 green cardamom pods, bruised
1 bay leaf
7.5cm/3in cinnamon stick
5ml/1 tsp black peppercorns
5ml/1 tsp cumin seeds
5ml/1 tsp coriander seeds

1 Put the rice in a colander and wash under cold running water until the water clears. Put in a bowl and pour 600ml/1 pint/2½ cups fresh water over the rice. Leave the rice to soak for 30 minutes; then drain thoroughly.

— COOK'S TIP —

You could add 2.5ml/½ tsp ground turmeric to the rice in step 2 of the recipe to colour it yellow.

2 Put the rice, salt and 600ml/ 1 pint/2½ cups water in a heavy-based pan. Bring to the boil, then cover and simmer for about 10 minutes. The rice should be just cooked with a little bite to it. Drain off any excess water, fluff up the grains with a fork, then spread it out on a tray and leave aside to cool.

3 Heat the ghee or butter in a wok until foaming, add the spices and stir-fry for 1 minute.

4 Add the cooled rice and stir-fry for 3–4 minutes until warmed through. Serve at once.

Thai Spring Rolls

These crunchy spring rolls are as popular in Thai cuisine as they are in the Chinese. Thais fill their version with a garlic, pork and noodle filling.

INGREDIENTS

Makes about 24
4–6 dried Chinese mushrooms, soaked
50g/2oz bean thread noodles, soaked
30ml/2 tbsp vegetable oil
2 garlic cloves, chopped
2 red chillies, seeded and chopped
225g/8oz minced pork
50g/2oz chopped cooked prawns
30ml/2 tbsp fish sauce
5ml/1 tsp granulated sugar
1 carrot, finely shredded
50g/2oz bamboo shoots, chopped
50g/2oz beansprouts
2 spring onions, chopped
15ml/1 tbsp chopped coriander
30ml/2 tbsp flour
24 x 15cm/6in square spring roll
   wrappers
freshly ground black pepper
oil for frying

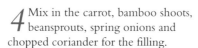

1 Drain and chop the mushrooms. Drain the noodles and cut into short lengths, about 5cm/2in.

2 Heat the oil in a wok or frying pan, add the garlic and chillies and fry for 30 seconds. Add the pork, stirring until the meat is browned.

3 Add the noodles, mushrooms and prawns. Season with fish sauce, sugar and pepper. Tip into a bowl.

4 Mix in the carrot, bamboo shoots, beansprouts, spring onions and chopped coriander for the filling.

5 Put the flour in a small bowl and mix with a little water to make a paste. Place a spoonful of filling in the centre of a spring roll wrapper.

6 Turn the bottom edge over to cover the filling, then fold in the left and right sides. Roll the wrapper up almost to the top edge. Brush the top edge with flour paste and seal. Repeat with the rest of the wrappers.

7 Heat the oil in a wok or deep-fat fryer. Slide in the spring rolls a few at a time and fry until crisp and golden brown. Remove with a slotted spoon and drain on kitchen paper. Serve hot with Thai sweet chilli sauce to dip them into, if liked.

Red Fried Rice

This vibrant rice dish owes its appeal as much to the bright colours of red onion, red pepper and cherry tomatoes as it does to their distinctive flavours.

INGREDIENTS

Serves 2

115g/4oz basmati rice
30ml/2 tbsp groundnut oil
1 small red onion, chopped
1 red pepper, seeded and chopped
225g/8oz cherry tomatoes, halved
2 eggs, beaten
salt and ground black pepper

1 Wash the rice several times under cold running water. Drain well. Bring a large pan of salted water to the boil, add the rice and cook for 10–12 minutes until tender.

2 Meanwhile, heat the oil in a wok until very hot. Add the onion and red pepper and stir-fry for 2–3 minutes. Add the cherry tomatoes and stir-fry for a further 2 minutes.

3 Pour in the beaten eggs all at once. Cook for 30 seconds without stirring, then stir to break up the egg as it sets.

4 Drain the cooked rice thoroughly, add to the wok and toss it over the heat with the vegetable and egg mixture for 3 minutes. Season the fried rice with salt and pepper to taste.

Vietnamese Spring Rolls with Nuoc Cham Sauce

INGREDIENTS

Makes 25

6 dried Chinese mushrooms, soaked
    in hot water for 30 minutes
225g/8oz lean ground pork
115g/4oz uncooked prawns, peeled,
    deveined and chopped
115g/4oz white crabmeat,
    picked over
1 carrot, shredded
50g/2oz cellophane noodles, soaked
    in water, drained and cut into
    short lengths
4 spring onions, finely sliced
2 garlic cloves, finely chopped
30ml/2 tbsp fish sauce
juice of 1 lime
freshly ground black pepper
25 x 10cm/4in Vietnamese
    rice sheets
oil for deep-frying
lettuce leaves, cucumber slices and
    coriander leaves, to garnish

For the nuoc cham sauce

2 garlic cloves, finely chopped
30ml/2 tbsp white wine vinegar
juice of 1 lime
30ml/2 tbsp sugar
120ml/4fl oz/½ cup fish sauce
120ml/4fl oz/½ cup water
2 red chillies, seeded and chopped

1 Drain the mushrooms, squeezing
out the excess moisture. Remove
the stems and thinly slice the caps
into a bowl. Add the pork, prawns,
crabmeat, carrot, cellophane noodles,
spring onions and garlic.

2 Season with the fish sauce, lime
juice and pepper. Set the mixture
aside for about 30 minutes to allow
the flavours to blend.

3 Meanwhile make the nuoc cham
sauce. Mix together the garlic,
vinegar, lime juice, sugar, fish sauce,
water and chillies in a serving bowl,
then cover and set aside.

4 Assemble the spring rolls. Place a
rice sheet on a flat surface and
brush with warm water until it is
pliable. Place about 10ml/2 tsp of the
filling near the edge of the rice sheet.
Fold the sides over the filling, fold in
the two ends, then roll up, sealing the
ends of the roll with a little water.
Make more rolls in the same way until
all the filling is used up.

5 Heat the oil for deep-frying to
180°C/350°F or until a cube of
dry bread added to the oil browns in
30–45 seconds. Add the rolls, a few at
a time, and fry until golden brown and
crisp. Drain on kitchen paper. Serve
the spring rolls hot, garnished with the
lettuce, cucumber and coriander. Offer
the nuoc cham sauce separately.

Fried Rice with Pork

If liked, garnish with strips of egg omelette.

INGREDIENTS

Serves 4–6

45ml/3 tbsp vegetable oil
1 onion, chopped
15ml/1 tbsp chopped garlic
115g/4oz pork, cut into small cubes
2 eggs, beaten
1kg/2¼lb/4 cups cooked rice
30ml/2 tbsp fish sauce
15ml/1 tbsp dark soy sauce
2.5 ml/½ tsp caster sugar
4 spring onions, finely sliced,
   to garnish
2 red chillies, sliced, to garnish
1 lime, cut into wedges, to garnish
egg omelette, to garnish (optional)

1 Heat the oil in a wok or large frying pan. Add the onion and garlic and cook for about 2 minutes until softened.

2 Add the pork to the softened onion and garlic. Stir-fry until the pork changes colour and is cooked.

3 Add the eggs and cook until scrambled into small lumps.

4 Add the rice and continue to stir and toss, to coat it with the oil and prevent it from sticking.

5 Add the fish sauce, soy sauce and sugar and mix well. Continue to fry until the rice is thoroughly heated. Garnish with sliced spring onion, red chillies and lime wedges. Top with a few strips of egg omelette, if using.

Chinese Crispy Spring Rolls

These small and dainty vegetarian stir-fried rolls are ideal served as starters or cocktail snacks. For a non-vegetarian, just replace the mushrooms with chicken or pork, and substitute prawns for the carrots.

INGREDIENTS

Makes 40 rolls

225g/8oz fresh bean sprouts
115g/4oz tender leeks or spring onions
115g/4oz carrots
115g/4oz bamboo shoots, sliced
115g/4oz white mushrooms
45–60ml/3–4 tbsp vegetable oil
5ml/1 tsp salt
5ml/1 tsp light brown sugar
15ml/1 tbsp light soy sauce
15ml/1 tbsp Chinese rice wine or
   dry sherry
20 frozen spring roll skins, thawed
15ml/1 tbsp cornflour paste
flour, for dusting
oil, for deep-frying
soy sauce, to serve (optional)

1 Cut all the vegetables into thin shreds, roughly the same size and shape as the bean sprouts.

COOK'S TIP

To make cornflour paste, mix 4 parts dry cornflour with about 5 parts cold water until smooth.

2 Heat the oil in a wok and stir-fry the vegetables for about 1 minute. Add the salt, sugar, soy sauce and rice wine or sherry and continue stirring for 1½ –2 minutes. Remove and drain the excess liquid, then leave to cool.

3 To make the spring rolls, cut each spring roll skin in half diagonally, then place about 15ml/1 tbsp of the vegetable mixture one third of the way down on the skin, with the triangle pointing away from you. Lift the lower flap over the filling and roll it up once.

4 Fold in both ends and roll once more, then brush the upper edge with a little cornflour paste, and roll into a neat pack. Lightly dust a tray with flour and place the spring rolls on the tray with the flap side down.

5 To cook, heat the oil in a wok until hot, then reduce the heat to low. Deep-fry the spring rolls in batches (about 8–10 at a time) for 2–3 minutes or until golden and crisp, then remove and drain. Serve the spring rolls hot with soy sauce, if using.

Special Fried Rice

Special fried rice is so substantial and tasty that it is another rice dish that is almost a meal in itself.

INGREDIENTS

Serves 4
50g/2oz peeled, cooked prawns
50g/2oz cooked ham
115g/4oz green peas
3 eggs
5ml/1 tsp salt
2 spring onions, finely chopped
60ml/4 tbsp vegetable oil
15ml/1 tbsp light soy sauce
15ml/1 tbsp Chinese rice wine or
   dry sherry
450g/1lb cooked rice

1 Pat dry the prawns with kitchen paper. Cut the ham into small dice about the same size as the peas.

2 In a bowl, lightly beat the eggs with a pinch of the salt and a few pieces of the spring onions.

3 Heat about half of the oil in a preheated wok, stir-fry the peas, prawns and ham for 1 minute, then add the soy sauce and rice wine or sherry. Remove and keep warm.

4 Heat the remaining oil in the wok and lightly scramble the eggs. Add the rice and stir to make sure that each grain of rice is separated. Add the remaining salt, spring onions and the prawns, ham and peas. Blend well and serve either hot or cold.

Butterfly Prawns

For best results, use uncooked giant or king prawns in their shells for this deep-fried dish. Sold headless, they are about 8–10cm/3–4in long, and you should get 18–20 prawns per 450g/1lb.

INGREDIENTS

Serves 6–8

450g/1lb uncooked prawns in their
   shells, headless
5ml/1 tsp ground Szechuan
   peppercorns
15ml/1 tbsp light soy sauce
15ml/1 tbsp Chinese rice wine or
   dry sherry
10ml/2 tsp cornflour
2 eggs, lightly beaten
60–75ml/4–5 tbsp breadcrumbs
vegetable oil, for deep-frying
2–3 spring onions, to garnish
lettuce leaves or crispy "seaweed",
   to serve

1 Peel the prawns but leave the tails on. Split the prawns in half from the underbelly, about three-quarters of the way through, leaving the tails still firmly attached.

2 Put the prawns in a bowl with the pepper, soy sauce, rice wine or sherry and cornflour and set aside to marinate for 10–15 minutes.

3 Pick up one prawn at a time by the tail, and dip it in the beaten egg.

4 Roll the egg-covered prawns in breadcrumbs.

5 Heat the oil in a wok until medium-hot. Gently lower the prawns into the oil.

6 Deep-fry the prawns in batches until golden brown. Remove and drain. Garnish with spring onions, which are either raw or have been soaked for about 30 seconds in hot oil. To serve, arrange the prawns neatly on a bed of lettuce leaves or crispy "seaweed".

Festive Rice

Nasi Kuning is served at special events – weddings, birthdays or farewell parties.

INGREDIENTS

Serves 8
450g/1lb Thai fragrant rice
60ml/4 tbsp oil
2 garlic cloves, crushed
2 onions, finely sliced
5cm/2in fresh turmeric, peeled and crushed
750ml/1¼ pints/3 cups water
400ml/14fl oz can coconut milk
1–2 lemon grass stems, bruised
1–2 *pandan* leaves (optional)
salt

For the accompaniments
omelette strips
2 fresh red chillies, shredded
cucumber chunks
tomato wedges
Deep-fried Onions
Coconut and Peanut Relish (optional)
prawn crackers

1 Wash the rice in several changes of water. Drain well.

2 Heat the oil in a wok and gently fry the crushed garlic, the finely sliced onions and the crushed fresh turmeric for a few minutes until soft but not browned.

COOK'S TIP

It is the custom to shape the rice into a cone (to represent a volcano) and then surround with the accompaniments. Shape with oiled hands or use a conical sieve.

3 Add the rice and and stir well so that each grain is thoroughly coated. Pour in the water and coconut milk and add the lemon grass, *pandan* leaves, if using, and salt.

4 Bring to the boil, stirring well. Cover and cook gently for about 15–20 minutes, until all of the liquid has been absorbed.

5 Remove from the heat. Cover with a dish towel, put on the lid and leave to stand in a warm place, for 15 minutes. Remove the lemon grass and *pandan* leaves.

6 Turn on to a serving platter and garnish with the accompaniments.

Quick-fried Prawns with Hot Spices

These spicy prawns are stir-fried in moments to make a wonderful starter. Don't forget that you will need to provide your guests with finger bowls.

INGREDIENTS

Serves 4

450g/1lb large raw prawns
2.5cm/1in fresh root ginger, grated
2 garlic cloves, crushed
5ml/1 tsp hot chilli powder
5ml/1 tsp ground turmeric
10ml/2 tsp black mustard seeds
seeds from 4 green cardamom
    pods, crushed
50g/2oz/4 tbsp ghee or butter
120ml/4fl oz/½ cup coconut milk
salt and ground black pepper
30–45ml/2–3 tbsp chopped fresh
    coriander, to garnish
naan bread, to serve

1 Peel the prawns carefully, leaving the tails attached.

2 Using a small sharp knife, make a slit along the back of each prawn and remove the dark vein. Rinse under cold running water, drain and pat dry.

3 Put the ginger, garlic, chilli powder, turmeric, mustard seeds and cardamom seeds in a bowl. Add the prawns and toss to coat completely with spice mixture.

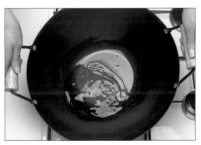

4 Heat a wok until hot. Add the ghee or butter and swirl it around until foaming.

5 Add the marinated prawns and stir-fry for 1–1½ minutes until they are just turning pink.

6 Stir in the coconut milk and simmer for 3–4 minutes until the prawns are just cooked through. Season to taste with salt and pepper. Sprinkle over the coriander and serve at once with naan bread.

Indonesian Fried Rice

This fried rice dish makes an ideal supper on its own or as an accompaniment to another dish.

INGREDIENTS

Serves 4–6

4 shallots, roughly chopped
1 fresh red chilli, seeded and chopped
1 garlic clove, chopped
thin sliver of dried shrimp paste
45ml/3 tbsp vegetable oil
225g/8oz boneless lean pork, cut into fine strips
175g/6oz long grain white rice, boiled and cooled
3–4 spring onions, thinly sliced
115g/4oz cooked peeled prawns
30ml/2 tbsp sweet soy sauce (*kecap manis*)
chopped fresh coriander and fine cucumber shreds, to garnish

1 In a mortar pound the shallots, chilli, garlic and shrimp paste with a pestle until they form a paste.

COOK'S TIP

Shrimp paste, sometimes called dried shrimp paste, is a strong-smelling and flavoursome paste made from fermented shrimps that is used extensively in many oriental cuisines. Always use sparingly. It is available from most oriental food stores and Chinese supermarkets.

2 Heat a wok until hot, add 30ml/ 2 tbsp of the oil and swirl it around. Add the pork and stir-fry for 2–3 minutes. Remove the pork from the wok, set aside and keep warm.

3 Add the remaining oil to the wok. When hot, add the spiced shallot paste and stir-fry for about 30 seconds.

4 Reduce the heat. Add the rice, sliced spring onions and prawns. Stir-fry for 2–3 minutes. Add the pork and sprinkle over the soy sauce. Stir-fry for 1 minute. Serve at once, garnished with chopped fresh coriander and cucumber shreds.

Deep-fried Ribs with Spicy Salt and Pepper

INGREDIENTS

Serves 4–6

10–12 finger ribs, about 675g/1½1b,
with excess fat and gristle trimmed
about 30–45ml/2–3 tbsp flour
vegetable oil, for deep-frying

For the marinade

1 clove garlic, crushed and
finely chopped
15ml/1 tbsp light brown sugar
15ml/1 tbsp light soy sauce
15ml/1 tbsp dark soy sauce
30ml/2 tbsp Chinese rice wine or
dry sherry
2.5ml/½ tsp chilli sauce
few drops sesame oil

For the spicy salt and pepper

15ml/1 tbsp salt
10ml/2 tsp ground Szechuan
peppercorns
5ml/1 tsp five-spice powder

1 Chop each rib into three or four
pieces, then mix with all the
marinade ingredients and marinate for
at least 2–3 hours.

2 Coat the ribs with flour and
deep-fry in medium-hot oil
for 4–5 minutes, stirring to separate.
Remove from the oil and drain.

— COOK'S TIP —

Ideally, each sparerib should be chopped
into three or four bitesize pieces before or
after deep-frying in a wok. If this is not
possible, then serve the ribs whole.

---

3 Heat the oil to high and deep-fry
the ribs once more for about
1 minute, or until the colour is an
even dark brown. Remove and drain.

4 To make the spicy salt and pepper,
heat all the ingredients in a
preheated dry wok for about 2 minutes
over a low heat, stirring constantly.
Serve with the ribs.

Chinese Jewelled Rice

This rice dish, with its many different, interesting ingredients, can make a meal in itself.

INGREDIENTS

Serves 4

350g/12oz long grain rice
45ml/3 tbsp vegetable oil
1 onion, roughly chopped
115g/4oz cooked ham, diced
175g/6oz canned white crab meat
75g/3oz canned water chestnuts,
   drained and cut into cubes
4 dried black Chinese mushrooms,
   soaked, drained and diced
115g/4oz peas, thawed if frozen
30ml/2 tbsp oyster sauce
5ml/1 tsp sugar
salt

1 Rinse the rice, then cook for 10–12 minutes in 700–900ml/ 1¼ –1½ pints/3–3¾ cups salted water in a saucepan with a tight-fitting lid. When cooked, refresh under cold water. Heat half the oil in a preheated wok, then stir-fry the rice for 3 minutes. Remove and set aside.

2 Add the remaining oil to the wok. When the oil is hot, cook the onion until softened but not coloured.

3 Add all the remaining ingredients and stir-fry for 2 minutes.

4 Return the rice to the wok and stir-fry for 3 minutes, then serve.

Deep-fried Squid with Spicy Salt and Pepper

This recipe is one of the specialities of the Cantonese school of cuisine. Southern China is famous for its seafood, often flavoured with ginger.

INGREDIENTS

Serves 4

450g/1lb squid
5ml/1 tsp ginger juice, see
 Cook's Tip
15ml/1 tbsp Chinese rice wine or
 dry sherry
about 575ml/1 pint/2½ cups
 boiling water
vegetable oil, for deep-frying
spicy salt and pepper
fresh coriander leaves, to garnish

1 Clean the squid by discarding the head and the transparent backbone as well as the ink bag; peel off and discard the thin skin, then wash the squid and dry well on kitchen paper. Open up the squid and, using a sharp knife, score the inside of the flesh in a criss-cross pattern.

2 Cut the squid into pieces, each about the size of a postage stamp. Marinate in a bowl with the ginger juice and rice wine or sherry for 25–30 minutes.

3 Blanch the squid in boiling water for a few seconds – each piece will curl up and the criss-cross pattern will open out to resemble ears of corn. Remove and drain. Dry well.

4 Heat sufficient oil for deep-frying in a wok. Deep-fry the squid for 15–20 seconds only, remove quickly and drain. Sprinkle with the spicy salt and pepper and serve garnished with fresh coriander leaves.

COOK'S TIP

To make ginger juice, mix finely chopped or grated fresh root ginger with an equal quantity of cold water and place in a piece of damp muslin. Twist tightly to extract the juice. Alternatively, crush the ginger in a garlic press.

Thai Fried Rice

This hot and spicy dish is easy to prepare and makes a complete meal in itself.

INGREDIENTS

Serves 4
225g/8oz Thai fragrant rice
45ml/3 tbsp vegetable oil
1 onion, chopped
1 small red pepper, seeded and cubed
   into 2cm/³/₄in cubes
350g/12oz skinless, boneless chicken
   breasts, cut into 2cm/³/₄in cubes.
1 garlic clove, crushed
15ml/1 tbsp mild curry paste
2.5ml/¹/₂ tsp paprika
2.5ml/¹/₂ tsp ground turmeric
30ml/2 tbsp Thai fish sauce
   (*nam pla*)
2 eggs, beaten
salt and ground black pepper
fried basil leaves, to garnish

2 Heat a wok until hot, add 30ml/ 2 tbsp of the oil and swirl it around. Add the onion and red pepper and stir-fry for 1 minute. Add the chicken cubes, garlic, curry paste and spices and stir-fry for 2–3 minutes.

3 Reduce the heat to medium, add the cooled rice, fish sauce and seasoning. Stir-fry for 2–3 minutes until the rice is very hot.

4 Make a well in the centre of the rice and add the remaining oil.

5 When hot, add the beaten eggs, leave to cook for about 2 minutes until lightly set, then stir into the rice.

6 Scatter over the fried basil leaves and serve at once.

1 Put the rice in a sieve and wash well under cold running water. Put the rice in a heavy-based pan with 1.5 litres/2½ pints/6¼ cups boiling water. Return to the boil, then simmer, uncovered, for 8–10 minutes; drain well. Spread out the grains on a tray and leave to cool.

— COOK'S TIP —

Thai fragrant rice has a particularly special fragrance and is generally served on feast days and other important occasions.

Spicy Meat-filled Parcels

In Indonesia the finest gossamer dough is made for *Martabak*. You can achieve equally good results using ready-made filo pastry or spring roll wrappers.

INGREDIENTS

Makes 16

450g/1lb lean minced beef
2 small onions, finely chopped
2 small leeks, very
   finely chopped
2 garlic cloves, crushed
10ml/2 tsp coriander seeds, dry-fried
   and ground
5ml/1 tsp cumin seeds, dry-fried
   and ground
5–10ml/1–2 tsp mild curry powder
2 eggs, beaten
400g/14oz packet filo pastry
45–60ml/3–4 tbsp sunflower oil
salt and freshly ground black pepper
light soy sauce, to serve

1 To make the filling, mix the meat with the onions, leeks, garlic, coriander, cumin, curry powder and seasoning. Turn into a heated wok, without oil, and stir all the time, until the meat has changed colour and looks cooked, about 5 minutes.

2 Allow to cool and then mix in enough beaten egg to bind to a soft consistency. Any leftover egg can be used to seal the edges of the dough; otherwise, use milk.

3 Brush a sheet of filo with oil and lay another sheet on top. Cut the sheets in half. Place a large spoonful of the filling on each double piece of filo. Fold the sides to the middle so that the edges just overlap. Brush these edges with either beaten egg or milk and fold the other two sides to the middle in the same way, so that you now have a square parcel shape. Make sure that the parcel is as flat as possible, to speed cooking. Repeat with the remaining fifteen parcels and place on a floured tray in the fridge.

4 Heat the remaining oil in a shallow pan and cook several parcels at a time, depending on the size of the pan. Cook for 3 minutes on the first side and then turn them over and cook for a further 2 minutes, or until heated through. Cook the remaining parcels in the same way and serve hot, sprinkled with light soy sauce.

5 If preferred, these spicy parcels can be cooked in a hot oven at 200°C/400°F/Gas 6 for 20 minutes. Glaze with more beaten egg before baking for a rich, golden colour.

Nasi Goreng

One of the most familiar and well-known Indonesian dishes. This is a marvellous way to use up leftover rice, chicken and meats such as pork. It is important that the rice is quite cold and the grains separate before adding the other ingredients, so it's best to cook the rice the day before.

INGREDIENTS

Serves 4–6

350g/12oz dry weight long grain rice, such as basmati, cooked and allowed to become completely cold
2 eggs
30ml/2 tbsp water
105ml/7 tbsp oil
225g/8oz pork fillet or fillet of beef
115g/4oz cooked, peeled prawns
175–225g/6–8oz cooked chicken, chopped
2–3 fresh red chillies, seeded and sliced
1cm/½in cube *terasi*
2 garlic cloves, crushed
1 onion, sliced
30ml/2 tbsp dark soy sauce or 45–60ml/3–4 tbsp tomato ketchup
salt and freshly ground black pepper
celery leaves, Deep-fried Onions and coriander sprigs, to garnish

2 Beat the eggs with seasoning and the water and make two or three omelettes in a frying pan, with a minimum of oil. Roll up each omelette and cut in strips when cold. Set aside.

3 Cut the pork or beef into neat strips and put the meat, prawns and chicken pieces in separate bowls. Shred one of the chillies and reserve it.

4 Put the *terasi*, with the remaining chilli, garlic and onion, in a food processor and grind to a fine paste. Alternatively, pound together using a pestle and mortar.

5 Fry the paste in the remaining hot oil, without browning, until it gives off a rich, spicy aroma. Add the pork or beef, tossing the meat all the time, to seal in the juices. Cook for 2 minutes, stirring constantly. Add the prawns, cook for 2 minutes and then stir in the chicken, cold rice, dark soy sauce or ketchup and seasoning to taste. Stir all the time to keep the rice light and fluffy and prevent it from sticking.

1 Once the rice is cooked and cooled, fork it through to separate the grains and keep it in a covered pan or dish until required.

6 Turn on to a hot platter and garnish with the omelette strips, celery leaves, onions, reserved shredded chilli and the coriander sprigs.

Hot Spicy Crab Claws

Crab claws are used to delicious effect in this quick stir-fried starter based on an Indonesian dish called *Kepiting Pedas*.

INGREDIENTS

Serves 4

12 fresh or frozen and thawed cooked
   crab claws
4 shallots, roughly chopped
2–4 fresh red chillies, seeded and
   roughly chopped
3 garlic cloves, roughly chopped
5ml/1 tsp grated fresh root ginger
2.5ml/$^1/_2$ tsp ground coriander
45ml/3 tbsp groundnut oil
60ml/4 tbsp water
10ml/2 tsp sweet soy sauce
   (*kecap manis*)
10–15ml/2–3 tsp lime juice
salt
fresh coriander leaves, to garnish

1 Crack the crab claws with the back of a heavy knife to make eating them easier and set aside. In a mortar, pound the chopped shallots with the pestle until pulpy. Add the chillies, garlic, ginger and ground coriander and pound until the mixture forms a fairly coarse paste.

2 Heat the wok over a medium heat. Add the oil and swirl it around. When it is hot, stir in the chilli paste. Stir-fry for about 30 seconds. Increase the heat to high. Add the crab claws and stir-fry for another 3–4 minutes.

3 Stir in the water, sweet soy sauce, lime juice and salt to taste. Continue to stir-fry for 1–2 minutes. Serve at once, garnished with fresh coriander. The crab claws are eaten with the fingers, so it is helpful to provide finger bowls.

— COOK'S TIP —

If whole crab claws are unavailable, look out for frozen ready-prepared crab claws. These are shelled with just the tip of the claw attached to the whole meat. Stir-fry for about 2 minutes until hot throughout.

Rice with Seeds and Spices

This dish provides a change from plain boiled rice, and is a colourful accompaniment to serve with curries or grilled meats.

INGREDIENTS

Serves 4

5ml/1 tsp sunflower oil
2.5ml/¹/₂ tsp ground turmeric
6 green cardamom pods,
  lightly crushed
5ml/1 tsp coriander seeds,
  lightly crushed
1 garlic clove, crushed
200g/7oz/1 cup basmati rice
400ml/14fl oz/1²/₃ cups stock
115g/4oz/¹/₂ cup natural yogurt
15ml/1 tbsp toasted sunflower seeds
15ml/1 tbsp toasted sesame seeds
salt and ground black pepper
coriander leaves, to garnish

1 Heat the oil in a non-stick frying pan and fry the spices and garlic for 1 minute, stirring constantly.

2 Add the rice and stock, bring to the boil, then cover and simmer for 15 minutes or until just tender.

3 Stir in the yogurt and the toasted sunflower and sesame seeds. Adjust the seasoning and serve the rice hot, garnished with coriander leaves.

Sweet Potato and Pumpkin Prawn Cakes

Serve these fried cakes warm with a fish sauce.

INGREDIENTS

Serves 4–6
200g/7oz strong white bread flour
2.5ml/½ tsp salt
2.5ml/½ tsp dried yeast
175ml/6fl oz/¾ cup hand-hot water
1 egg, beaten
200g/7oz fresh prawn tails, peeled and
    roughly chopped
150g/5oz sweet potato, peeled
    and grated
225g/8oz pumpkin, peeled, seeded
    and grated
2 spring onions, chopped
50g/2oz water chestnuts, sliced
    and chopped
2.5ml/½ tsp chilli sauce
1 clove garlic, crushed
juice of ½ lime
30–45ml/2–3 tbsp vegetable oil
spring onions, to garnish

1 Sift the flour and salt into a mixing bowl and make a well in the centre. Dissolve the yeast in the water, then pour into the well. Pour in the egg and leave for a few minutes until bubbles appear. Mix to a batter.

2 Place the peeled prawns in a saucepan and cover with water. Bring to the boil and simmer for 10–12 minutes. Drain, refresh in cold water and drain again. Roughly chop and set the prawns aside.

3 Add the sweet potato and pumpkin to the batter, then add the spring onions, water chestnuts, chilli sauce, garlic, lime juice and prawns. Heat a little oil in a wok or frying pan. Spoon in the batter in small heaps and fry until golden. Drain and serve, garnished with spring onions.

RICE DISHES

Not just one of the world's staples, but one of its favourites too, rice is among the most useful store-cupboard ingredients, providing an easy accompaniment at a few moments' notice or the basis of a main-meal dish in hardly any more time. It is the perfect starting point for an amazing range of tastes and flavours when combined with a variety of other delicious ingredients. It should not be forgotten that many different types of rice — all with their own distinctive flavours, textures and characteristics — are available to enhance your meal.

Fish Cakes with Cucumber Relish

These wonderful small fish cakes are a very familiar and popular appetizer. They are usually accompanied with Thai beer.

INGREDIENTS

Makes about 12

300g/11oz white fish fillet, such as cod, cut into chunks
30ml/2 tbsp red curry paste
1 egg
30ml/2 tbsp fish sauce
5ml/1 tsp granulated sugar
30ml/2 tbsp cornflour
3 kaffir lime leaves, shredded
15ml/1 tbsp chopped coriander
50g/2oz green beans, finely sliced
oil for frying
Chinese mustard cress, to garnish

For the cucumber relish

60ml/4 tbsp Thai coconut or rice vinegar
60ml/4 tbsp water
50g/2oz sugar
1 head pickled garlic
1 cucumber, quartered and sliced
4 shallots, finely sliced
15ml/1 tbsp finely chopped root ginger
2 red chillies, seeded and finely sliced

1 To make the cucumber relish, bring the vinegar, water and sugar to the boil. Stir until the sugar dissolves, then remove from the heat and cool.

2 Combine the rest of the relish ingredients together in a bowl and pour over the vinegar mixture.

3 Combine the fish, curry paste and egg in a food processor and process well. Transfer the mixture to a bowl, add the rest of the ingredients, except for the oil and garnish, and mix well.

4 Mould and shape the mixture into cakes about 5cm/2in in diameter and 5mm/¼in thick.

5 Heat the oil in a wok or deep-fat fryer. Fry the fish cakes, a few at a time, for about 4–5 minutes or until golden brown. Remove and drain on kitchen paper. Garnish with Chinese mustard cress and serve with the cucumber relish.

Stir-fried Tofu and Beansprouts with Noodles

This is a satisfying dish, which is both tasty and easy to make.

INGREDIENTS

Serves 4

225g/8oz firm tofu
groundnut oil, for deep-frying
175g/6oz medium egg noodles
15ml/1 tbsp sesame oil
5ml/1 tsp cornflour
10ml/2 tsp dark soy sauce
30ml/2 tbsp Chinese rice wine or
  dry sherry
5ml/1 tsp sugar
6–8 spring onions, cut diagonally into
  2.5cm/1in lengths
3 garlic cloves, sliced
1 fresh green chilli, seeded and sliced
115g/4oz Chinese cabbage leaves,
  roughly shredded
50g/2oz beansprouts
50g/2oz toasted cashew nuts, to garnish

1 Drain the tofu and pat dry with kitchen paper. Cut the tofu into 2.5cm/1in cubes. Half-fill a wok with groundnut oil and heat to 180°C/350°F. Deep-fry the tofu in batches for 1–2 minutes until golden and crisp. Drain on kitchen paper. Carefully pour all but 30ml/2 tbsp of the oil from the wok.

2 Cook the noodles. Rinse them thoroughly under cold water and drain well. Toss them in 10ml/2 tsp of the sesame oil and set aside. In a bowl, blend together the cornflour, soy sauce, rice wine or sherry, sugar and remaining sesame oil.

3 Reheat the 30ml/2 tbsp of groundnut oil and, when hot, add the spring onions, garlic, chilli, Chinese cabbage and beansprouts. Stir-fry for 1–2 minutes.

4 Add the tofu with the noodles and sauce. Cook, stirring, for about 1 minute until well mixed. Sprinkle over the cashew nuts. Serve at once.

Spiced Honey Chicken Wings

Be prepared to get very sticky when you eat these stir-fried wings, as the best way to enjoy them is by eating them with your fingers. Provide individual finger bowls for your guests.

INGREDIENTS

Serves 4
1 red chilli, finely chopped
5ml/1 tsp chilli powder
5ml/1 tsp ground ginger
rind of 1 lime, finely grated
12 chicken wings
60ml/4 tbsp sunflower oil
15ml/1 tbsp fresh coriander, chopped
30ml/2 tbsp soy sauce
50ml/3$\frac{1}{2}$ tbsp clear honey
lime rind and fresh coriander sprigs,
   to garnish

1 Mix the fresh chilli, chilli powder, ground ginger and lime rind together. Rub the mixture into the chicken skins and leave for at least 2 hours to allow the flavours to penetrate.

2 Heat a wok and add half the oil. When the oil is hot, add half the wings and stir-fry for 10 minutes, turning regularly until crisp and golden. Drain on kitchen paper. Repeat with the remaining oil and chicken wings.

3 Add the coriander to the hot wok and stir-fry for 30 seconds, then return the wings to the wok and stir-fry for 1 minute.

4 Stir in the soy sauce and honey, and stir-fry for 1 minute. Serve the chicken wings hot with the sauce drizzled over them and garnished with lime rind and coriander sprigs.

Noodles with Ginger and Coriander

Here is a simple noodle dish that goes well with most oriental dishes. It can also be served as a snack for two or three people.

INGREDIENTS

Serves 4–6
handful fresh coriander sprigs
225g/8oz dried egg noodles
45ml/3 tbsp groundnut oil
5cm/2in fresh root ginger,
   finely shredded
6–8 spring onions, shredded
30ml/2 tbsp light soy sauce
salt and ground black pepper

COOK'S TIP

Many of the dried egg noodles available are sold packed in layers. As a guide, allow 1 layer of noodles per person as an average portion for a main dish.

1 Strip the leaves from the coriander sprigs. Pile them on a chopping board and chop them roughly, using a cleaver or large sharp knife.

2 Cook the noodles according to the packet instructions. Rinse under cold water and drain well. Toss them in 15ml/1 tbsp of the oil.

3 Heat a wok until hot, add the remaining oil and swirl it around. Add the ginger and stir-fry for a few seconds, then add the noodles and spring onions. Stir-fry for 3–4 minutes until hot.

4 Sprinkle over the soy sauce, coriander and seasoning. Toss well, then serve at once.

Bon-bon Chicken with Sesame Sauce

The chicken meat is tenderized by being beaten with a stick (called a *bon* in Chinese), hence the name for this very popular Szechuan dish.

INGREDIENTS

Serves 6–8
1 chicken, about 1kg/2¼lb
1.2 litre/2 pints/5 cups water
15ml/1 tbsp sesame oil
shredded cucumber, to garnish

For the sauce
30ml/2 tbsp light soy sauce
5ml/1 tsp sugar
15ml/1 tbsp finely chopped
   spring onions
5ml/1 tsp red chilli oil
2.5ml/½ tsp ground Szechuan
   peppercorns
5ml/1 tsp white sesame seeds
30ml/2 tbsp sesame paste or 30ml/
   2 tbsp peanut butter creamed with
   a little sesame oil

1 Clean the chicken well. Bring the water to a rolling boil in a wok, add the chicken. Reduce the heat, cover and cook for 40–45 minutes. Remove the chicken and immerse in cold water to cool.

2 After at least 1 hour, remove the chicken and drain; dry well with kitchen paper and brush on a coating of sesame oil. Carve the meat off the legs, wings and breast and pull the meat off the rest of the bones.

3 On a flat surface, pound the meat with a rolling pin, then tear the meat into shreds with your fingers.

4 Place the meat in a dish with the shredded cucumber around the edge. In a bowl, mix together all the sauce ingredients, keeping a few spring onions to garnish. Pour the sauce over the chicken and serve.

Fried Noodles with Beansprouts and Asparagus

Soft fried noodles contrast beautifully with crisp beansprouts and asparagus.

INGREDIENTS

Serves 4

115g/4oz dried egg noodles
60ml/4 tbsp vegetable oil
1 small onion, chopped
2.5cm/1in fresh root ginger, peeled and grated
2 garlic cloves, crushed
175g/6oz young asparagus spears, trimmed
115g/4oz beansprouts
4 spring onions, sliced
45ml/3 tbsp soy sauce
salt and ground black pepper

1 Bring a pan of salted water to the boil. Add the noodles and cook for 2–3 minutes, until tender. Drain and toss them in 30ml/2 tbsp of the oil.

2 Heat the remaining oil in a preheated wok until very hot. Add the onion, ginger and garlic and stir-fry for 2–3 minutes. Add the asparagus and stir-fry for a further 2–3 minutes.

3 Add the noodles and beansprouts and stir-fry for 2 minutes.

4 Stir in the spring onions and soy sauce. Season to taste, adding salt sparingly as the soy sauce will add quite a salty flavour. Stir-fry for 1 minute, then serve at once.

FISH AND SHELLFISH

Rapid stir-frying is ideally suited to cooking fish and shellfish as it helps to retain the light texture and delicate flavour. This has long been an open secret in India, China and South-east Asia, whose cuisines have inspired many of the scrumptious recipes here, including seafood Balti with vegetables, fish balls with Chinese greens, Malaysian fish curry, and oriental scallops with ginger relish. A wok is also the perfect piece of equipment for braising whole fish or fillets and for preparing pastes, flavourings and sauces to accompany fish.

Noodles with Asparagus and Saffron Sauce

A rather elegant summery dish with fragrant saffron cream.

INGREDIENTS

Serves 4
450g/1lb young asparagus
pinch of saffron threads
25g/1oz butter
2 shallots, finely chopped
30ml/2 tbsp white wine
250ml/8fl oz/1 cup double cream
grated rind and juice of ½ lemon
115g/4oz peas
350g/12oz somen noodles
½ bunch chervil, roughly chopped
salt and freshly ground black pepper
grated Parmesan cheese (optional)

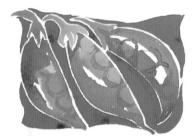

1 Cut off the asparagus tips (about 5cm/2in in length), then slice the remaining spears into short rounds. Steep the saffron in 30ml/2 tbsp boiling water in a cup.

2 Melt the butter in a saucepan, add the shallots and cook over a low heat for 3 minutes until soft. Add the white wine, cream and saffron infusion. Bring to the boil, reduce the heat and simmer gently for 5 minutes or until the sauce thickens to a coating consistency. Add the grated lemon rind and juice, with salt and pepper to taste.

3 Bring a large saucepan of lightly salted water to the boil. Blanch the asparagus tips, scoop them out and add them to the sauce, then cook the peas and short asparagus rounds in the boiling water until just tender. Scoop them out and add to the sauce.

4 Cook the somen noodles in the same water until just tender, following the directions on the packet. Drain, place in a wide pan and pour the sauce over the top.

5 Toss the noodles with the sauce and vegetables, adding the chervil and more salt and pepper if needed. Finally, sprinkle with the grated Parmesan, if using, and serve hot.

Fish Balls with Chinese Greens

These tasty fish balls are steamed over a wok with a selection of green vegetables – pak choi is available from oriental stores.

INGREDIENTS

Serves 4

For the fish balls

450g/1lb white fish fillets, skinned, boned and cubed
3 spring onions, chopped
1 back bacon rasher, rinded and chopped
15ml/1 tbsp Chinese rice wine
30ml/2 tbsp light soy sauce
1 egg white

For the vegetables

1 small head pak choi
5ml/1 tsp cornflour
15ml/1 tbsp light soy sauce
150ml/^{1}/$_4$ pint/^{2}/$_3$ cup cup fish stock
30ml/2 tbsp groundnut oil
2 garlic cloves, sliced
2.5cm/1in fresh root ginger, cut into thin shreds
75g/3oz green beans
175g/6oz mangetouts
3 spring onions, sliced diagonally into 5–7.5cm/2–3in lengths
salt and ground black pepper

1 Put the fish, spring onions, bacon, rice wine, soy sauce and egg white in a food processor and process until smooth. With wetted hands, form the mixture into about 24 small balls.

2 Steam the fish balls in batches in a lightly greased bamboo steamer in a wok for 5–10 minutes until cooked through and firm. Remove from the steamer and keep warm.

3 Meanwhile trim the pak choi, removing any discoloured leaves or damaged stems, then tear into manageable pieces.

4 Blend together the cornflour, soy sauce and stock in a small bowl and set aside.

5 Heat a wok until hot, add the oil and swirl it around. Add the garlic and ginger and stir-fry for 2–3 minutes. Add the beans and stir-fry for 2–3 minutes, then add the mangetouts, spring onions and pak choi. Stir-fry for 2–3 minutes.

6 Add the sauce to the wok and cook, stirring, until it has thickened and the vegetables are tender but crisp. Taste and adjust the seasoning, if necessary. Serve with the fish balls.

Mixed Rice Noodles

A delicious noodle dish made extra special by adding avocado and garnishing with prawns.

INGREDIENTS

Serves 4

15ml/1 tbsp sunflower oil
2.5cm/1in fresh root ginger, peeled and grated
2 cloves garlic, crushed
45ml/3 tbsp dark soy sauce
225g/8oz peas, thawed if frozen
450g/1lb rice noodles
450g/1lb spinach, stalks removed
30ml/2 tbsp smooth peanut butter
30ml/2 tbsp tahini
150ml/¼ pint/⅔ cup milk
1 ripe avocado, peeled and stoned
roasted peanuts and peeled, cooked prawns, to garnish

1 Heat the wok, then add the oil. When the oil is hot, stir-fry the ginger and garlic for 30 seconds. Add 15ml/1 tbsp of the soy sauce and 150ml/¼ pint/⅔ cup boiling water.

--- COOK'S TIP ---

Do not peel, stone or slice the avocado much in advance of using as the flesh quickly discolours. Sprinkling with a little lemon or lime juice helps prevent this.

2 Add the peas and noodles, then cook for 3 minutes. Stir in the spinach. Remove the vegetables and noodles, drain and keep warm.

3 Stir the peanut butter, remaining soy sauce, tahini and milk together in the wok, and simmer for 1 minute.

4 Add the vegetables and noodles, slice in the avocado and toss together. Serve piled on individual plates. Spoon some sauce over each portion and garnish with roasted peanuts and prawns.

Thai Fish Stir-fry

This is a substantial dish, best served with crusty bread, for mopping up all the spicy juices.

INGREDIENTS

Serves 4

675g/1¹/₂lb mixed seafood, such as red snapper and cod, filleted and skinned, and raw prawn tails
300ml/¹/₂ pint/1¹/₄ cups coconut milk
15ml/1 tbsp vegetable oil
salt and ground black pepper
crusty bread, to serve

For the sauce
2 large red fresh chillies
1 onion, roughly chopped
5cm/2in fresh root ginger, peeled and sliced
5cm/2in lemon grass stalk, outer leaf discarded, roughly sliced
5cm/2in piece galangal peeled and sliced
6 blanched almonds, chopped
2.5ml/¹/₂ tsp turmeric
2.5ml/¹/₂ tsp salt

1 Cut the filleted fish into large chunks. Peel the prawns, keeping their tails intact.

COOK'S TIP

Galangal, also spelt galingale, is a rhizome from the same family as ginger, with a similar but milder flavour. It is peeled and sliced, chopped or grated in the same way as root ginger. It is an important spice in South-east Asian cooking, particularly in Indonesia, Malaysia and Thailand.

2 To make the sauce, carefully remove the seeds from the chillies and chop the flesh roughly. Put the chillies and the other sauce ingredients in a food processor or blender with 45ml/3 tbsp of the coconut milk. Process until smooth.

3 Heat a wok, then add the oil. When the oil is hot, stir-fry the seafood for 2–3 minutes, then remove.

4 Add the sauce and the remaining coconut milk to the wok, then return the seafood. Bring to the boil, season well and serve with crusty bread.

Noodles with Sun-dried Tomatoes and Prawns

INGREDIENTS

Serves 4

350g/12oz somen noodles
45ml/3 tbsp olive oil
20 uncooked king prawns, peeled
    and deveined
2 garlic cloves, finely chopped
45–60ml/3–4 tbsp sun-dried
    tomato paste
salt and freshly ground black pepper

For the garnish
handful of basil leaves
30ml/2 tbsp sun-dried tomatoes in oil,
    drained and cut into strips

--- COOK'S TIP ---

Ready-made sun-dried tomato paste is readily available, however you can make your own simply by processing bottled sun-dried tomatoes with their oil. You could also add a couple of anchovy fillets and some capers if you like.

1 Cook the noodles in a large saucepan of boiling water until tender, following the directions on the packet. Drain.

2 Heat half the oil in a large frying pan. Add the prawns and garlic and fry them over a medium heat for 3–5 minutes, until the prawns turn pink and are firm to the touch.

3 Stir in 15ml/1 tbsp of the sun-dried tomato paste and mix well. Using a slotted spoon, transfer the prawns to a bowl and keep hot.

4 Reheat the oil remaining in the pan. Stir in the rest of the oil with the remaining sun-dried tomato paste. You may need to add a spoonful of water if the mixture is very thick.

5 When the mixture starts to sizzle, toss in the noodles. Add salt and pepper to taste and mix well.

6 Return the prawns to the pan and toss to combine. Serve at once garnished with the basil and strips of sun-dried tomatoes.

Karahi Prawns and Fenugreek

The black-eyed beans, prawns and paneer in this mean that it is rich in protein. The combination of both ground and fresh fenugreek makes this a very fragrant and delicious dish.

INGREDIENTS

Serves 4–6

60ml/4 tbsp corn oil
2 onions, sliced
2 medium tomatoes, sliced
7.5ml/1½ tsp garlic pulp
5ml/1 tsp chilli powder
5ml/1 tsp ginger pulp
5ml/1 tsp ground cumin
5ml/1 tsp ground coriander
5ml/1 tsp salt
150g/5oz paneer, cubed
5ml/1 tsp ground fenugreek
1 bunch fresh fenugreek leaves
115g/4oz cooked prawns
2 fresh red chillies, sliced
30ml/2 tbsp chopped fresh coriander
50g/2oz canned black-eyed
  beans, drained
15ml/1 tbsp lemon juice

1 Heat the oil in a preheated wok. Lower the heat slightly and add the onions and tomatoes. Fry, stirring occasionally, for about 3 minutes.

2 Add the garlic, chilli powder, ginger, ground cumin, ground coriander, salt, paneer and the ground and fresh fenugreek. Lower the heat and stir-fry for about 2 minutes.

3 Add the prawns, red chillies, fresh coriander and the black-eyed beans and mix well. Cook for a further 3–5 minutes, stirring occasionally, or until the prawns are heated through.

4 Finally sprinkle over the lemon juice and serve.

Bamie Goreng

This fried noodle dish is wonderfully accommodating. To the basic recipe you can add other vegetables, such as mushrooms, tiny pieces of chayote, broccoli, leeks or beansprouts, if you prefer. As with fried rice, you can use whatever you have to hand, bearing in mind the need to achieve a balance of colours, flavours and textures.

INGREDIENTS

Serves 6–8
450g/1lb dried egg noodles
1 boneless, skinless chicken breast
115g/4oz pork fillet
115g/4oz calves' liver (optional)
2 eggs, beaten
90ml/6 tbsp oil
25g/1oz butter or margarine
2 garlic cloves, crushed
115g/4oz cooked, peeled prawns
115g/4oz spinach or Chinese leaves
2 celery sticks, finely sliced
4 spring onions, shredded
about 60ml/4 tbsp chicken stock
dark soy sauce and light soy sauce
salt and freshly ground black pepper
Deep-fried Onions and celery leaves,
    to garnish

2 Finely slice the chicken, pork fillet and calves' liver, if using.

4 Heat the remaining oil in a wok and fry the garlic with the chicken, pork and liver for 2–3 minutes, until they have changed colour. Add the prawns, spinach or Chinese leaves, celery and spring onions, tossing well.

5 Add the cooked and drained noodles and toss well again so that all the ingredients are well mixed. Add enough stock just to moisten and dark and light soy sauce to taste. Finally, stir in the scrambled eggs.

1 Cook the noodles in salted, boiling water for 3–4 minutes. Drain, rinse with cold water and drain again. Set aside until required.

3 Season the eggs. Heat 5ml/1 tsp oil with the butter or margarine in a small pan until melted and then stir in the eggs and keep stirring until scrambled. Set aside.

6 Garnish the dish with Deep-fried Onions and celery leaves.

Paneer Balti with Prawns

Although paneer is not widely eaten in Pakistan, it makes an excellent substitute for red meat. Here it is combined with king prawns to make a memorable stir-fry dish.

INGREDIENTS

Serves 4

12 cooked king prawns
175g/6oz paneer
30ml/2 tbsp tomato purée
60ml/4 tbsp Greek-style yogurt
7.5ml/1½ tsp garam masala
5ml/1 tsp chilli powder
5ml/1 tsp garlic pulp
5ml/1 tsp salt
10ml/2 tsp mango powder
5ml/1 tsp ground coriander
115g/4oz butter
15ml/1 tbsp corn oil
3 fresh green chillies, chopped
45ml/3 tbsp chopped fresh coriander
150ml/¼ pint/⅔ cup single cream

1 Peel the king prawns and cube the paneer. Blend together the tomato purée, yogurt, garam masala, chilli powder, garlic, salt, mango powder and ground coriander in a mixing bowl and set aside.

2 Melt the butter with the oil in a wok. Lower the heat slightly and stir-fry the paneer and prawns for about 2 minutes. Remove with a slotted spoon and drain on kitchen paper. Set aside.

3 Pour the spice mixture into the butter and oil left in the pan and stir-fry for about 1 minute.

4 Add the paneer and prawns, and cook for 7–10 minutes, stirring occasionally, until the prawns are heated through.

5 Add the fresh chillies and most of the coriander, and pour in the cream. Heat through for about 2 minutes, garnish with the remaining fresh coriander and serve.

COOK'S TIP

To make paneer at home, bring 1 litre/1¾ pints/4 cups milk to the boil over a low heat. Add 30ml/2 tbsp lemon juice, stirring continuously and gently until the milk thickens and begins to curdle. Strain the curdled milk through a sieve lined with muslin. Set aside under a heavy weight for about 1½–2 hours to press to a flat shape about 1cm/½in thick.

Make the paneer a day before you plan to use it in a recipe; it will then be firmer and easier to handle. Cut and use as required; it will keep for about one week in the refrigerator.

Thai Fried Noodles

Phat Thai has a fascinating flavour and texture. It is made with rice noodles and is considered one of the national dishes of Thailand.

INGREDIENTS

Serves 4–6
350g/12oz rice noodles
45ml/3 tbsp vegetable oil
15ml/1 tbsp chopped garlic
16 uncooked king prawns, shelled, tails
  left intact and deveined
2 eggs, lightly beaten
15ml/1 tbsp dried shrimps, rinsed
30ml/2 tbsp pickled white radish
50g/2oz fried bean curd, cut into
  small slivers
2.5ml/½ tsp dried chilli flakes
115g/4oz garlic chives, cut into
  5cm/2in lengths
225g/8oz beansprouts
50g/2oz roasted peanuts, coarsely
  ground
5ml/1 tsp granulated sugar
15ml/1 tbsp dark soy sauce
30ml/2 tbsp fish sauce
30ml/2 tbsp tamarind juice
30ml/2 tbsp coriander leaves,
  to garnish
1 kaffir lime, to garnish

1 Soak the noodles in warm water for 20–30 minutes, then drain.

2 Heat 15ml/1 tbsp of the oil in a wok or large frying pan. Add the garlic and fry until golden. Stir in the prawns and cook for about 1–2 minutes until pink, tossing from time to time. Remove and set aside.

3 Heat another 15ml/1 tbsp of oil in the wok. Add the eggs and tilt the wok to spread them into a thin sheet. Stir to scramble and break the egg into small pieces. Remove from the wok and set aside with the prawns.

4 Heat the remaining oil in the same wok. Add the dried shrimps, pickled radish, bean curd and dried chillies. Stir briefly. Add the soaked noodles and stir-fry for 5 minutes.

5 Add the garlic chives, half the beansprouts and half the peanuts. Season with the granulated sugar, soy sauce, fish sauce and tamarind juice. Mix well and cook until the noodles are heated through.

6 Return the prawn and egg mixture to the wok and mix with the noodles. Serve garnished with the rest of the beansprouts, peanuts, coriander leaves and lime wedges.

Boemboe Bali of Fish

The island of Bali has wonderful fish, surrounded as it is by sparkling blue sea. This simple fish "curry" is packed with many of the characteristic flavours associated with Indonesia.

INGREDIENTS

Serves 4–6

675g/1½lb cod or haddock fillet
1cm/½in cube *terasi*
2 red or white onions
2.5cm/1in fresh root ginger, peeled and sliced
1cm/½in fresh *lengkuas*, peeled and sliced, or 5ml/1 tsp *lengkuas* powder
2 garlic cloves
1–2 fresh red chillies, seeded, or 5–10ml/1–2 tsp chilli powder
90ml/6 tbsp sunflower oil
15ml/1 tbsp dark soy sauce
5ml/1 tsp tamarind pulp, soaked in 30ml/2 tbsp warm water
250ml/8fl oz/1 cup water
celery leaves or chopped fresh chilli, to garnish
boiled rice, to serve

1 Skin the fish, remove any bones and then cut the flesh into bitesize pieces. Pat dry with kitchen paper and set aside.

2 Grind the *terasi*, onions, ginger, *lengkuas*, garlic and fresh chillies, if using, to a paste in a food processor or with a pestle and mortar. Stir in the chilli powder and *lengkuas* powder, if using.

3 Heat 30ml/2 tbsp of the oil and fry the spice mixture, stirring, until it gives off a rich aroma. Add the soy sauce. Strain the tamarind and add the juice and water. Cook for 2–3 minutes.

— VARIATION —

Substitute 450g/1lb cooked tiger prawns. Add them 3 minutes before the end.

---

4 In a separate pan, fry the fish in the remaining oil for 2–3 minutes. Turn once only so that the pieces stay whole. Lift out with a draining spoon and put into the sauce.

5 Cook the fish in the sauce for a further 3 minutes and serve with boiled rice. Garnish the dish with feathery celery leaves or a little chopped fresh chilli, if liked.

Stir-fried Rice Noodles with Chicken and Prawns

Shellfish have a natural affinity with both meat and poultry. This Thai-style recipe combines chicken with prawns and has the characteristic sweet, sour and salty flavour.

INGREDIENTS

Serves 4

225g/8oz dried flat rice noodles
120ml/4fl oz/½ cup water
60ml/4 tbsp fish sauce
15ml/1 tbsp sugar
15ml/1 tbsp fresh lime juice
5ml/1 tsp paprika
pinch of cayenne pepper
45ml/3 tbsp oil
2 garlic cloves, finely chopped
1 skinless, boneless chicken breast, finely sliced
8 raw prawns, peeled, deveined and cut in half
1 egg
50g/2oz roasted peanuts, coarsely crushed
3 spring onions, cut into short lengths
175g/6oz beansprouts
coriander leaves and 1 lime, cut into wedges, to garnish

1 Place the rice noodles in a large bowl, cover with warm water and soak for 30 minutes until soft. Drain.

2 Combine the water, fish sauce, sugar, lime juice, paprika and cayenne in a small bowl. Set aside until required.

3 Heat the oil in a wok. Add the garlic and fry for 30 seconds until it starts to brown. Add the chicken and prawns and stir-fry for 3–4 minutes until cooked.

4 Push the chicken and prawn mixture in the wok out to the sides. Break the egg into the centre, then quickly stir to break up the yolk and cook over a medium heat until the egg is just lightly scrambled.

5 Add the drained noodles and the fish sauce mixture to the wok. Mix together well. Add half the crushed peanuts and cook, stirring frequently, until the noodles are soft and most of the liquid has been absorbed.

6 Add the spring onions and half of the beansprouts. Cook, stirring for 1 minute more. Spoon on to a platter. Sprinkle with the remaining peanuts and beansprouts. Garnish with the coriander and lime wedges and serve.

Braised Whole Fish in Chilli and Garlic Sauce

This is a classic Szechuan recipe. When it is served in a restaurant, the fish's head and tail are usually discarded before cooking, and used in other dishes. A whole fish may be used, however, and always looks impressive, especially for special occasions and formal dinner parties.

INGREDIENTS

Serves 4–6

1 carp, bream, sea bass, trout, grouper or grey mullet, weighing about 675g/1½lb, gutted
15ml/1 tbsp light soy sauce
15ml/1 tbsp Chinese rice wine or dry sherry
vegetable oil, for deep-frying

For the sauce
2 cloves garlic, finely chopped
2–3 spring onions, finely chopped with the white and green parts separated
5ml/1 tsp finely chopped fresh root ginger
30ml/2 tbsp chilli bean sauce
15ml/1 tbsp tomato purée
10ml/2 tsp light brown sugar
15ml/1 tbsp rice vinegar
120ml/4fl oz/½ cup chicken stock
15ml/1 tbsp cornflour paste
few drops of sesame oil

1 Rinse and dry the fish well. Using a sharp knife, score both sides of the fish down to the bone with diagonal cuts about 2.5cm/1in apart. Rub both sides of the fish with the soy sauce and rice wine or sherry. Set aside for 10–15 minutes to marinate.

2 Heat sufficient oil for deep-frying in a wok. When it is hot, add the fish and fry for 3–4 minutes on both sides, until golden brown.

3 To make the sauce pour away all but about 15ml/1 tbsp of the oil. Push the fish to one side of the wok and add the garlic, the white part of the spring onions, the ginger, chilli bean sauce, tomato purée, sugar, vinegar and stock. Bring to the boil and braise the fish in the sauce for 4–5 minutes, turning it over once. Add the green of the spring onions. Stir in the cornflour paste to thicken the sauce. Sprinkle over a little sesame oil and serve.

Noodles with Meatballs

Mie Rebus is a one-pot meal, for which the East is renowned. It's fast food, served from street stalls.

INGREDIENTS

Serves 6

450g/1lb Spicy Meatball mixture
350g/12oz dried egg noodles
45ml/3 tbsp sunflower oil
1 large onion, finely sliced
2 garlic cloves, crushed
2.5cm/1in fresh root ginger, peeled and
   cut in thin matchsticks
1.2 litres/2 pints/5 cups stock
30ml/2 tbsp dark soy sauce
2 celery sticks, finely sliced,
   leaves reserved
6 Chinese leaves, cut in bitesize pieces
1 handful mangetouts, cut in strips
salt and freshly ground black pepper

1 Prepare the meatballs, making them quite small. Set aside.

2 Add the noodles to a large pan of salted, boiling water and stir so that the noodles do not settle at the bottom. Simmer for 3–4 minutes, or until *al dente*. Drain in a colander and rinse with plenty of cold water. Set aside.

3 Heat the oil in a wide pan and fry the onion, garlic and ginger until soft but not browned. Add the stock and soy sauce and bring to the boil.

4 Add the meatballs, half-cover and allow to simmer until they are cooked, about 5–8 minutes depending on size. Just before serving, add the sliced celery and, after 2 minutes, add the Chinese leaves and mangetouts. Taste and adjust the seasoning.

5 Divide the noodles among soup bowls, add the meatballs and vegetables and pour the soup on top. Garnish with the reserved celery leaves.

Seafood Balti with Vegetables

The spicy seafood is cooked separately and combined with vegetables at the last minute.

INGREDIENTS

Serves 4

For the seafood

225g/8oz cod, or any other firm, white fish
225g/8 oz peeled, cooked prawns
6 crab sticks, halved lengthways
15ml/1 tbsp lemon juice
5ml/1 tsp ground coriander
5ml/1 tsp chilli powder
5ml/1 tsp salt
5ml/1 tsp ground cumin
60ml/4 tbsp cornflour
150ml/¼ pint/⅔ cup corn oil

For the vegetables

150ml/¼ pint/⅔ cup corn oil
2 onions, chopped
5ml/1 tsp onion seeds
½ cauliflower, cut into florets
115g/4oz French beans, cut into 2.5cm/1in lengths
175g/6oz sweetcorn
5ml/1 tsp shredded fresh root ginger
5ml/1 tsp chilli powder
5ml/1 tsp salt
4 fresh green chillies, sliced
30ml/2 tbsp chopped fresh coriander
lime slices, to garnish (optional)

1 Skin the fish and cut into small cubes. Put it into a mixing bowl with the prawns and crab sticks.

COOK'S TIP

Raita makes a delicious accompaniment to this seafood dish. Whisk 300ml/½ pint/ 1¼ cups natural yogurt, then whisk in 120ml/4 fl oz/½ cup water. Stir in 5ml/ 1 tsp salt, 30ml/2 tbsp chopped fresh coriander and 1 finely chopped green chilli. Garnish with slices of cucumber and one or two sprigs of mint.

---

2 In a separate bowl, mix together the lemon juice, ground coriander, chilli powder, salt and ground cumin. Pour this over the seafood and mix together thoroughly using your hands.

3 Sprinkle on the cornflour and mix again until the seafood is well coated. Set aside in the refrigerator for about 1 hour to allow the flavours to develop fully.

4 To make the vegetable mixture, heat the oil in a preheated wok. Add the onions and the onion seeds and stir-fry until lightly browned.

5 Add the cauliflower, French beans, sweetcorn, ginger, chilli powder, salt, green chillies and fresh coriander. Stir-fry for about 7–10 minutes over a medium heat, making sure that the cauliflower florets retain their shape.

6 Spoon the fried vegetables around the edge of a shallow dish, leaving a space in the middle for the seafood, and keep warm.

7 Wash and dry the pan, then heat the oil to fry the seafood pieces. Fry the seafood pieces in two or three batches, until they turn a golden brown. Remove with a slotted spoon and drain on kitchen paper.

8 Arrange each batch of seafood in the middle of the dish of vegetables and keep warm while you fry the remaining batches. Garnish with lime slices, if using, and serve immediately.

Buckwheat Noodles with Smoked Trout

The light, crisp texture of the bok choy balances the earthy flavours of the mushrooms, the buckwheat noodles and the smokiness of the trout.

INGREDIENTS

Serves 4

350g/12oz buckwheat noodles
30ml/2 tbsp vegetable oil
115g/4oz fresh shiitake
   mushrooms, quartered
2 garlic cloves, finely chopped
15ml/1 tbsp grated fresh
   root ginger
225g/8oz bok choy
1 spring onion, finely
   sliced diagonally
15ml/1 tbsp dark sesame oil
30ml/2 tbsp mirin
30ml/2 tbsp soy sauce
2 smoked trout, skinned and boned
salt and freshly ground black pepper
30ml/2 tbsp coriander leaves and
   10ml/2 tsp sesame seeds, toasted,
   to garnish

1 Cook the buckwheat noodles in a saucepan of boiling water for about 7–10 minutes or until just tender, following the directions on the packet.

2 Meanwhile heat the oil in a large frying pan. Add the shiitake mushrooms and sauté over a medium heat for 3 minutes. Add the garlic, ginger and bok choy, and continue to sauté for 2 minutes.

3 Drain the noodles and add them to the mushroom mixture with the spring onion, sesame oil, mirin and soy sauce. Toss and season with salt and pepper to taste.

4 Break the smoked trout in bite-size pieces. Arrange the noodle mixture on individual serving plates. Place the smoked trout on top of the noodles.

5 Garnish the noodles with coriander leaves and sesame seeds and serve them immediately.

Balti Fish Fillets in Spicy Coconut Sauce

Use fresh fish fillets to make this dish if you can, as they have much more flavour than frozen ones. However, if you are using frozen fillets, ensure that they are completely thawed before using.

INGREDIENTS

Serves 4

30ml/2 tbsp corn oil
5ml/1 tsp onion seeds
4 dried red chillies
3 garlic cloves, sliced
1 onion, sliced
2 tomatoes, sliced
30ml/2 tbsp desiccated coconut
5ml/1 tsp salt
5ml/1 tsp ground coriander
4 flatfish fillets, such as plaice, sole or
    flounder, each about 75g/3oz
150ml/¼ pint/⅔ cup water
15ml/1 tbsp lime juice
15ml/1 tbsp chopped fresh coriander
boiled rice, to serve (optional)

1 Heat the oil in a wok. Lower the heat slightly and add the onion seeds, dried red chillies, garlic slices and onion. Cook for 3–4 minutes, stirring once or twice.

2 Add the tomatoes, coconut, salt and coriander and stir thoroughly.

3 Cut each fish fillet into three pieces. Drop the fish pieces into the mixture and turn them over gently until they are well coated.

4 Cook for 5–7 minutes, lowering the heat if necessary. Add the water, lime juice and fresh coriander and cook for a further 3–5 minutes until the water has mostly evaporated. Serve immediately with rice, if using.

COOK'S TIP

The Balti equivalent of the Chinese wok is the karahi, also known as a Balti pan. They are usually round-bottomed with two carrying handles. Like the wok, the karahi is traditionally made of cast iron in order to withstand the high temperatures and hot oil used in cooking. They are now made in a variety of different metals and are available in a range of sizes, including small ones for individual servings.

Rice Noodles with Beef and Black Bean Sauce

This is an excellent combination – beef with a chilli sauce tossed with silky smooth rice noodles.

INGREDIENTS

Serves 4

450g/1lb fresh rice noodles
60ml/4 tbsp vegetable oil
1 onion, finely sliced
2 garlic cloves, finely chopped
2 slices fresh root ginger,
   finely chopped
225g/8oz mixed peppers, seeded and
   cut into strips
350g/12oz rump steak, finely sliced
   against the grain
45ml/3 tbsp fermented black beans,
   rinsed in warm water, drained
   and chopped
30ml/2 tbsp soy sauce
30ml/2 tbsp oyster sauce
15ml/1 tbsp chilli black bean sauce
15ml/1 tbsp cornflour
120ml/4fl oz/½ cup stock or water
2 spring onions, finely chopped, and
   2 red chillies, seeded and finely
   sliced, to garnish

1 Rinse the noodles under hot water; drain well. Heat half the oil in a wok or large frying pan, swirling it around. Add the onion, garlic, ginger and mixed pepper strips. Stir-fry for 3–5 minutes, then remove with a slotted spoon and keep hot.

2 Add the remaining oil to the wok. When hot, add the sliced beef and fermented black beans and stir-fry over a high heat for 5 minutes or until they are cooked.

3 In a small bowl, blend the soy sauce, oyster sauce and chilli black bean sauce with the cornflour and stock or water until smooth. Add the mixture to the wok, then return the onion mixture to the wok and cook, stirring, for 1 minute.

4 Add the noodles and mix lightly. Stir over a medium heat until the noodles are heated through. Adjust the seasoning if necessary. Serve at once, garnished with the chopped spring onions and chillies.

Thai Fish Cakes

Bursting with flavours of chillies, lime and lemon grass, these little fish cakes make a wonderful starter or light lunch dish.

INGREDIENTS

Serves 4
450g/1lb white fish fillets, such as cod or haddock
3 spring onions, sliced
30ml/2 tbsp chopped fresh coriander
30ml/2 tbsp Thai red curry paste
1 fresh green chilli, seeded and chopped
10ml/2 tsp grated lime rind
15ml/1 tbsp lime juice
30ml/2 tbsp groundnut oil
salt
crisp lettuce leaves, shredded spring onions, fresh red chilli slices, coriander sprigs and lime wedges, to serve

1 Cut the fish into chunks, then place them in a blender or food processor.

2 Add the spring onions, coriander, red curry paste, green chilli, lime rind and juice to the fish. Season with salt. Process until finely minced.

3 Using lightly floured hands, divide the mixture into 16 pieces and shape each one into a small cake about 4cm/1½in across. Place the fish cakes on a plate, cover with clear film and chill for about 2 hours until firm.

4 Heat a wok over a high heat until hot. Add the oil and swirl it around. Fry the fish cakes, a few at a time, for 6–8 minutes, turning them over carefully until evenly browned. Drain each batch on kitchen paper and keep hot while you are cooking the remainder. Serve on a bed of crisp lettuce leaves with shredded spring onions, red chilli slices, fresh coriander sprigs and lime wedges.

Fried Singapore Noodles

Thai fish cakes add a wonderful spiciness to this stir-fry. Make them yourself or buy them from an oriental supermarket. They vary quite considerably in size and degree of spiciness.

INGREDIENTS

Serves 4

175g/6oz rice noodles
60ml/4 tbsp vegetable oil
2.5ml/½ tsp salt
75g/3oz cooked prawns
175g/6oz cooked pork, cut
  into matchsticks
1 green pepper, seeded and chopped
  into matchsticks
2.5ml/½ tsp sugar
10ml/2 tsp curry powder
75g/3oz Thai fish cakes
10ml/2 tsp dark soy sauce

1 Soak the rice noodles in water for about 10 minutes, drain well, then pat dry with kitchen paper.

COOK'S TIP

Rice noodles, called *banh trang*, are made from ground rice and water. They range in thickness from very thin to wide ribbons and sheets. Dried ribbon rice noodles are usually sold tied together in bundles. Fresh rice noodles are also available. Both can be bought from oriental food stores.

2 Heat the wok, then add half the oil. When the oil is hot, add the noodles and half the salt and stir-fry for 2 minutes. Transfer to a heated serving dish and keep warm.

3 Heat the remaining oil and add the prawns, pork, pepper, sugar, curry powder and remaining salt. Stir-fry for 1 minute. Return the noodles to the wok and stir-fry with the Thai fish cakes for 2 minutes. Stir in the soy sauce and serve at once.

Spiced Salmon Stir-fry

Marinating the salmon allows all the flavours to develop, and the lime juice tenderizes the fish beautifully, so it needs very little stir-frying – be careful not to overcook it.

INGREDIENTS

Serves 4

4 salmon steaks, about 225g/8oz each
4 whole star anise
2 lemon grass stalks, sliced
juice of 3 limes
rind of 3 limes, finely grated
30ml/2 tbsp clear honey
30ml/2 tbsp grapeseed oil
salt and ground black pepper
lime wedges, to garnish

1 Remove the middle bone from each steak, using a very sharp filleting knife, to make two strips from each steak.

2 Remove the skin by inserting the knife at the thin end of each piece of salmon. Sprinkle 5ml/1 tsp salt on the cutting board to prevent the fish slipping while removing the skin. Slice into pieces, cutting diagonally.

3 Roughly crush the star anise in a mortar with a pestle. Place the salmon in a non-metallic dish and add the star anise, lemon grass, lime juice and rind and honey. Season well with salt and pepper. Turn the salmon strips to coat. Cover and leave in the refrigerator to marinate overnight.

4 Carefully drain the salmon from the marinade, pat dry on kitchen paper and reserve the marinade.

5 Heat a wok, then add the oil. When the oil is hot, add the salmon and stir-fry, stirring constantly until cooked. Increase the heat, pour over the marinade and bring to the boil. Garnish with lime wedges and serve.

COOK'S TIP

Star anise contains the same oil as the more familiar Mediterranean spice, anise or aniseed, but looks completely different. Its star-shaped pods are particularly attractive, so it is often used whole in Chinese cooking for its decorative effect. It is also becoming increasingly popular with western cooks for the same reason. It is an essential ingredient in many classic Chinese recipes and is one of the spices that constitute five-spice powder. The flavour of star anise is very strong and liquorice-tasting with rather deeper undertones than its European counterpart.

Mee Krob

This delicious dish makes a filling meal. Take care when frying rice vermicelli in the wok as it has a tendency to spit when added to hot oil.

INGREDIENTS

Serves 4

120ml/4fl oz/½ cup vegetable oil
225g/8oz rice vermicelli
150g/5oz French beans, topped, tailed
    and halved lengthways
1 onion, finely chopped
2 boneless, skinless chicken breasts,
    about 175g/6oz each, cut into strips
5ml/1 tsp chilli powder
225g/8oz cooked prawns
45ml/3 tbsp dark soy sauce
45ml/3 tbsp white wine vinegar
10ml/2 tsp caster sugar
fresh coriander sprigs, to garnish

1 Heat the wok, then add 60ml/ 4 tbsp of the oil. Break up the vermicelli into 7.5cm/3in lengths. When the oil is hot, fry the vermicelli in batches. Remove from the heat and keep warm.

2 Heat the remaining oil in the wok, then add the French beans, onion and chicken and stir-fry for 3 minutes until the chicken is cooked.

3 Sprinkle in the chilli powder. Stir in the prawns, soy sauce, vinegar and sugar, and stir-fry for 2 minutes.

4 Serve the chicken, prawns and vegetables piled on the fried vermicelli, garnished with sprigs of fresh coriander.

— COOK'S TIP —

There is little consensus about chilli powder. Some varieties consist purely of ground, dried, hot chillies, whereas others are a mixture of ground chillies and various other spices and herbs, including oregano and cumin. The latter is more suitable for Mexican cuisine than for use in oriental dishes. In any case, pure ground chilli is a more sensible choice as you can include your own additional flavourings if you want to, but you cannot lose any that are already there. Some chilli powders even include cheaper, "bulking" ingredients, so it is always sensible to read the label carefully before buying. This will also give some indication of how mild or hot the spice is. To be absolutely sure of quality, you can grind your own chilli powder from dried chillies in a mortar with a pestle. Wear rubber gloves to protect your hands and avoid touching your eyes or mouth.

Chunky Fish Balti with Peppers

Try to find as many different colours of peppers as possible to make this very attractive dish.

INGREDIENTS

Serves 2–4

450g/1lb cod or any other firm, white fish
7.5ml/1½ tsp ground cumin
10ml/2 tsp mango powder
5ml/1 tsp ground coriander
2.5ml/½ tsp chilli powder
5ml/1 tsp salt
5ml/1 tsp ginger pulp
45ml/3 tbsp cornflour
150ml/¼ pint/⅔ cup corn oil
1 each green, orange and red peppers, seeded and chopped
8–10 cherry tomatoes, to garnish

1 Skin the fish, then cut it into small cubes. Put the cubes into a large mixing bowl and add the ground cumin, mango powder, ground coriander, chilli powder, salt, ginger and cornflour. Mix together thoroughly until the fish is well coated.

2 Heat the oil in a wok. When it is hot, lower the heat slightly and add the fish pieces, three or four at a time. Fry for about 3 minutes, turning them and stirring constantly.

3 Drain the fish pieces on kitchen paper and transfer them to a serving dish. Keep warm while you fry the remaining fish pieces.

4 Fry the peppers in the remaining oil for about 2 minutes. They should still be slightly crisp. Drain on kitchen paper.

5 Add the cooked peppers to the fish on the serving dish and garnish with the cherry tomatoes.

COOK'S TIP

This dish is delicious when served with raita and paratha, a traditional Balti unleavened bread with rich flaky layers.

Fried Cellophane Noodles

INGREDIENTS

Serves 4

175g/6oz cellophane noodles
45ml/3 tbsp vegetable oil
3 garlic cloves, finely chopped
115g/4oz cooked prawns, peeled
2 lap cheong, rinsed, drained and
   finely diced
2 eggs
2 celery sticks, including leaves, diced
115g/4oz beansprouts
115g/4oz spinach, cut into
   large pieces
2 spring onions, chopped
15–30ml/1–2 tbsp fish sauce
5ml/1 tsp sesame oil
15ml/1 tbsp sesame seeds, toasted,
   to garnish

1 Soak the cellophane noodles in hot water for about 10 minutes or until soft. Drain and cut the noodles into 10cm/4in lengths.

2 Heat the oil in a wok, add the garlic and fry until golden brown. Add the prawns and lap cheong; stir-fry for 2–3 minutes. Stir in the noodles and fry for 2 minutes more.

3 Make a well in the centre of the prawn mixture, break in the eggs and slowly stir them until they are creamy and just set.

--- COOK'S TIP ---

This is a very versatile dish. Vary the vegetables if you wish and substitute ham, chorizo or salami for the lap cheong.

4 Stir in the celery, beansprouts, spinach and spring onions. Season with fish sauce and stir in the sesame oil. Continue to stir-fry until all the ingredients are cooked, mixing well.

5 Transfer to a serving dish. Sprinkle with sesame seeds to garnish.

Sweet and Sour Fish

When fish is cooked in this way the skin becomes crispy on the outside, while the flesh remains moist and juicy inside. The sweet and sour sauce, with its colourful cherry tomatoes, complements the fish beautifully.

INGREDIENTS

Serves 4–6

1 large or 2 medium-size fish such as
   snapper or mullet, heads removed
20ml/4 tsp cornflour
120ml/4fl oz/½ cup vegetable oil
15ml/1 tbsp chopped garlic
15ml/1 tbsp chopped root ginger
30ml/2 tbsp chopped shallots
225g/8oz cherry tomatoes
30ml/2 tbsp red wine vinegar
30ml/2 tbsp granulated sugar
30ml/2 tbsp tomato ketchup
15ml/1 tbsp fish sauce
45ml/3 tbsp water
salt and freshly ground black pepper
coriander leaves, to garnish
shredded spring onions, to garnish

1 Thoroughly rinse and clean the fish. Score the skin diagonally on both sides of the fish.

2 Coat the fish lightly on both sides with 15ml/1 tbsp cornflour. Shake off any excess.

3 Heat the oil in a wok or large frying pan and slide the fish into the wok. Reduce the heat to medium and fry the fish until crisp and brown, about 6–7 minutes on both sides.

4 Remove the fish with a fish slice and place on a large platter.

5 Pour off all but 30ml/2 tbsp of the oil and add the garlic, ginger and shallots. Fry until golden.

6 Add the cherry tomatoes and cook until they burst open. Stir in the vinegar, sugar, tomato ketchup and fish sauce. Simmer gently for 1–2 minutes and adjust the seasoning.

7 Blend the remaining 5ml/1 tsp cornflour with the water. Stir into the sauce and heat until it thickens. Pour the sauce over the fish and garnish with coriander leaves and shredded spring onions.

Vegetarian Fried Noodles

When making this dish for non-vegetarians, or for vegetarians who eat fish, add a piece of *blacan* (compressed shrimp paste). A small chunk about the size of a stock cube, mashed with the chilli paste, will add a deliciously rich, aromatic flavour.

INGREDIENTS

Serves 4

2 eggs
5ml/1 tsp chilli powder
5ml/1 tsp turmeric
60ml/4 tbsp vegetable oil
1 large onion, finely sliced
2 red chillies, seeded and
   finely sliced
15ml/1 tbsp soy sauce
2 large cooked potatoes, cut into
   small cubes
6 pieces fried bean curd, sliced
225g/8oz beansprouts
115g/4oz green beans, blanched
350g/12oz fresh thick egg noodles
salt and freshly ground black pepper
sliced spring onions, to garnish

1 Beat the eggs lightly, then strain them into a bowl. Heat a lightly greased omelette pan. Pour in half of the egg to cover the bottom of the pan thinly. When the egg is just set, turn the omelette over and fry the other side briefly. Slide on to a plate, blot with kitchen paper, roll up and cut into narrow strips. Make a second omelette in the same way and slice. Set the omelette strips aside for the garnish.

COOK'S TIP

Always be very careful when handling chillies. Keep your hands away from your eyes as chillies will sting them. Wash your hands thoroughly after touching chillies.

2 In a cup, mix together the chilli powder and turmeric. Form a paste by stirring in a little water.

3 Heat the oil in a wok or large frying pan. Fry the onion until soft. Reduce the heat and add the chilli paste, sliced chillies and soy sauce. Fry for 2–3 minutes.

4 Add the potatoes and fry for about 2 minutes, mixing well with the chillies. Add the bean curd, then the beansprouts, green beans and noodles.

5 Gently stir-fry until the noodles are evenly coated and heated through. Take care not to break up the potatoes or the bean curd. Season with salt and pepper. Serve hot, garnished with the reserved omelette strips and spring onion slices.

Malaysian Fish Curry

Fish gently cooked in a wok of coconut milk makes a mouth-watering curry for any occasion.

INGREDIENTS

Serves 4–6

675g/1¹/₂lb monkfish, hokey or
   red snapper fillet
salt, to taste
45ml/3 tbsp grated or
   desiccated coconut
30ml/2 tbsp vegetable oil
2.5cm/1in galangal or fresh root ginger,
   peeled and thinly sliced
2 small red chillies, seeded and
   finely chopped
2 cloves garlic, crushed
5cm/2in lemon grass stalk, shredded
1 piece shrimp paste, 1cm/¹/₂in square
   or 15ml/1 tbsp fish sauce
400g/14oz canned coconut milk
600ml/1 pint/2¹/₂ cups chicken stock
2.5ml/¹/₂ tsp turmeric
15ml/1 tbsp sugar
juice of 1 lime, or ¹/₂ lemon
boiled rice, to serve (optional)

1 Cut the fish into large chunks, season with salt and set aside.

COOK'S TIP

Sambal, a fiery hot relish, is traditionally served with this curry. Mix together 2 skinned and chopped tomatoes, 1 finely chopped onion, 1 finely chopped green chilli and 30ml/2 tbsp lime juice. Season to taste with salt and pepper and sprinkle over 30ml/2 tbsp grated or desiccated coconut.

2 Dry-fry the coconut in a large wok until evenly brown. Add the vegetable oil, galangal or ginger, chillies, garlic and lemon grass and fry briefly. Stir in the shrimp paste or fish sauce. Strain the coconut milk through a sieve, then add to the wok.

3 Add the chicken stock, turmeric, sugar, a little salt and the lime or lemon juice. Simmer for 10 minutes. Add the fish and simmer for 6–8 minutes. Stir in the thick part of the coconut milk and simmer to thicken. Garnish with coriander and lime slices and serve with rice, if using.

Chicken Chow Mein

Chow Mein is arguably the best known Chinese noodle dish in the West. Noodles are stir-fried with meat, seafood or vegetables.

INGREDIENTS

Serves 4

350g/12oz noodles
225g/8oz skinless, boneless
  chicken breasts
45ml/3 tbsp soy sauce
15ml/1 tbsp rice wine or dry sherry
15ml/1 tbsp dark sesame oil
60ml/4 tbsp vegetable oil
2 garlic cloves, finely chopped
50g/2oz mange-touts, topped
  and tailed
115g/4oz beansprouts
50g/2oz ham, finely shredded
4 spring onions, finely chopped
salt and freshly ground black pepper

1 Cook the noodles in a saucepan of boiling water until tender. Drain, rinse under cold water and drain well.

2 Slice the chicken into fine shreds about 5cm/2in in length. Place in a bowl and add 10ml/2 tsp of the soy sauce, the rice wine or sherry and sesame oil.

3 Heat half the vegetable oil in a wok or large frying pan over a high heat. When it starts smoking, add the chicken mixture. Stir-fry for 2 minutes, then transfer the chicken to a plate and keep it hot.

4 Wipe the wok clean and heat the remaining oil. Stir in the garlic, mange-touts, beansprouts and ham, stir-fry for another minute or so and add the noodles.

5 Continue to stir-fry until the noodles are heated through. Add the remaining soy sauce to taste and season with salt and pepper. Return the chicken and any juices to the noodle mixture, add the chopped spring onions and give the mixture a final stir. Serve at once.

Vinegar Fish

Fish cooked in a spicy mixture that includes chillies, ginger and vinegar is an Indonesian speciality. It is a method that lends itself particularly well to strong-flavoured, oily fish, such as the mackerel used here.

INGREDIENTS

Serves 2–3

2–3 mackerel, filleted
2-3 red chillies, seeded
4 macadamia nuts or 8 almonds
1 red onion, quartered
2 garlic cloves, crushed
1cm/½in piece root ginger, peeled
   and sliced
5ml/1 tsp ground turmeric
45ml/3 tbsp coconut or vegetable oil
45ml/3 tbsp wine vinegar
150ml/¼ pint/⅔ cup water
salt
deep-fried onions and finely chopped
   chilli, to garnish
boiled or coconut rice, to
   serve (optional)

1 Rinse the mackerel fillets in cold water and dry well on kitchen paper. Set aside.

COOK'S TIP

To make coconut rice, put 400g/14oz washed long grain rice in a heavy saucepan with 2.5ml/½ tsp salt, a 5cm/2in piece of lemon grass and 25g/1oz creamed coconut. Add 750ml/1¼ pints/3 cups boiling water and stir once to prevent the grains sticking together. Simmer over a medium heat for 10–12 minutes. Remove the pan from the heat, cover and set aside for 5 minutes. Fluff the rice with a fork or chopsticks before serving.

2 Put the chillies, macadamia nuts or almonds, onion, garlic, ginger, turmeric and 15ml/1 tbsp of the oil in a food processor and process to form a paste. Alternatively, pound them together in a mortar with a pestle to form a paste. Heat the remaining oil in a wok. When it is hot, add the paste and cook for 1–2 minutes without browning. Stir in the vinegar and water and season with salt to taste. Bring to the boil, then lower the heat.

3 Add the mackerel fillets to the sauce and simmer for 6–8 minutes or until the fish is tender and cooked.

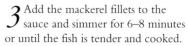

4 Transfer the fish to a warm serving dish. Bring the sauce to a boil and cook for 1 minute or until it has reduced slightly. Pour the sauce over the fish, garnish with the deep-fried onions and chopped chilli and serve with rice, if using.

Special Chow Mein

Lap cheong is a special air-dried Chinese sausage. It is available from most Chinese supermarkets. If you cannot buy it, substitute with either diced ham, chorizo or salami.

INGREDIENTS

Serves 4–6

45ml/3 tbsp vegetable oil
2 garlic cloves, sliced
5ml/1 tsp chopped fresh root ginger
2 red chillies, chopped
2 lap cheong, about 75g/3oz, rinsed
  and sliced (optional)
1 boneless chicken breast, thinly sliced
16 uncooked tiger prawns, peeled, tails
  left intact, and deveined
115g/4oz green beans
225g/8oz beansprouts
50g/2oz garlic chives
450g/1lb egg noodles, cooked in
  boiling water until tender
30ml/2 tbsp soy sauce
15ml/1 tbsp oyster sauce
salt and freshly ground black pepper
15ml/1 tbsp sesame oil
2 spring onions, shredded, to garnish
15ml/1 tbsp coriander leaves,
  to garnish

1 Heat 15ml/1 tbsp of the oil in a wok or large frying pan and fry the garlic, ginger and chillies. Add the lap cheong, if using, chicken, prawns and beans. Stir-fry for about 2 minutes over a high heat or until the chicken and prawns are cooked. Transfer the mixture to a bowl and set aside.

2 Heat the rest of the oil in the same wok. Add the beansprouts and garlic chives. Stir fry for 1–2 minutes.

4 Return the prawn mixture to the wok. Reheat and mix well with the noodles. Stir in the sesame oil. Serve garnished with spring onions and coriander leaves.

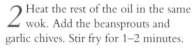

3 Add the noodles and toss and stir to mix. Season with soy sauce, oyster sauce, salt and pepper.

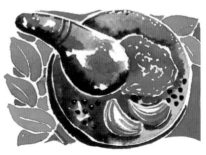

Fragrant Swordfish with Ginger and Lemon Grass

Swordfish is a firm-textured, meaty fish which cooks well in a wok if it has been marinated as steaks rather than cut in strips. It is sometimes a little dry, but this is counteracted by the marinade. If you cannot get swordfish, use any variety of fresh tuna.

INGREDIENTS

Serves 4

1 kaffir lime leaf
45ml/3 tbsp rock salt
75ml/5 tbsp brown sugar
4 swordfish steaks, about 225g/
 8oz each
1 lemon grass stalk, sliced
2.5cm/1in fresh root ginger, cut
 into matchsticks
1 lime
15ml/1 tbsp grapeseed oil
1 large ripe avocado, peeled and stoned
salt and ground black pepper

1 Bruise the lime leaf by crushing slightly, to release the flavour.

─────── COOK'S TIP ───────

Kaffir lime leaves are intensely aromatic with a distinctive figure-of-eight shape. They are used extensively in Indonesian and Thai cooking, and Thai cuisine also makes use of the fruit rind of the lime from this particular type of tree.

2 To make the marinade, process the rock salt, brown sugar and lime leaf together in a food processor or blender until thoroughly blended.

3 Place the swordfish steaks in a bowl. Sprinkle the marinade over them and add the lemon grass and root ginger matchsticks. Leave for 3–4 hours to marinate.

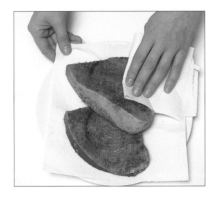

4 Rinse off the marinade and pat the fish dry with kitchen paper.

5 Peel the lime. Remove any excess pith from the peel. Cut the peel into very thin strips. Squeeze the juice from the fruit.

6 Heat a wok, then add the oil. When the oil is hot, add the lime rind and then the swordfish steaks. Stir-fry for 3–4 minutes. Add the lime juice. Remove the wok from the heat, slice the avocado and add to the fish. Season to taste and serve.

NOODLES

There are many different sorts of noodles, and the ways in which they can be served are virtually endless because they combine so well with almost all other ingredients. For the busy cook, they have the added advantage of being both quick and easy to prepare. The recipes here have been inspired by the cuisines of many countries, sometimes marrying western and oriental flavours in inventive dishes. Discover the versatility of noodles with dishes such as buckwheat noodles with smoked trout, noodles with meatballs, or bamie goreng.

Green Curry of Prawns

A popular fragrant creamy curry that also takes very little time to prepare. It can also be made with thin strips of chicken meat.

INGREDIENTS

Serves 4–6

30ml/2 tbsp vegetable oil
30ml/2 tbsp green curry paste
450g/1lb king prawns, shelled
   and deveined
4 kaffir lime leaves, torn
1 stalk lemon grass, bruised
   and chopped
250ml/8fl oz/1 cup coconut milk
30ml/2 tbsp fish sauce
½ cucumber, seeded and cut into thin
   batons
10–15 basil leaves
4 green chillies, sliced, to garnish

1 Heat the oil in a frying pan. Add the green curry paste and fry until bubbling and fragrant.

2 Add the prawns, kaffir lime leaves and lemon grass. Fry for 1–2 minutes, until the prawns are pink.

3 Stir in the coconut milk and bring to a gentle boil. Simmer, stirring occasionally, for about 5 minutes or until the prawns are tender.

4 Stir in the fish sauce, cucumber, and basil, then top with the green chillies and serve.

Larp of Chiang Mai

Chiang Mai is a city in the north-east of Thailand. The city is culturally very close to Laos and famous for its chicken salad, which was originally called "Laap" or "Larp". Duck, beef or pork can be used instead.

INGREDIENTS

Serves 4–6
450g/1lb minced chicken
1 stalk lemon grass, finely chopped
3 kaffir lime leaves, finely chopped
4 red chillies, seeded and chopped
60ml/4 tbsp lime juice
30ml/2 tbsp fish sauce
15ml/1 tbsp roasted ground rice
2 spring onions, chopped
30ml/2 tbsp coriander leaves
mixed salad leaves, cucumber and
    tomato slices, to serve
a few sprigs of mint, to garnish

1 Heat a large non-stick frying pan. Add the minced chicken and cook in a little water.

COOK'S TIP

Use sticky, or glutinous, rice to make roasted ground rice. Put the rice in a frying pan and dry-roast until golden brown. Remove and grind to a powder in a pestle and mortar or in a food processor. Keep in a glass jar in a cool and dry place and use as required.

2 Stir constantly until cooked; this will take about 7–10 minutes.

3 Transfer the cooked chicken to a large bowl and add the rest of the ingredients. Mix thoroughly.

4 Serve on a bed of mixed salad leaves, cucumber and tomato slices and garnish with sprigs of mint.

Stir-fried Prawns with Broccoli

This is a very colourful dish, highly nutritious and at the same time extremely delicious; furthermore, it is not time-consuming or difficult to prepare.

INGREDIENTS

Serves 4

175–225g/6–8oz prawns, shelled and deveined
5ml/1 tsp salt
15ml/1 tbsp Chinese rice wine or dry sherry
$^1/_2$ egg white
15ml/1 tbsp cornflour paste
225g/8oz broccoli
about 300ml/$^1/_2$ pint/1$^1/_4$ cups vegetable oil
1 spring onion, cut into short sections
5ml/1 tsp light brown sugar
about 30ml/2 tbsp stock or water
5ml/1 tsp light soy sauce
few drops sesame oil

1 Cut each prawn in half lengthways. Mix with a pinch of salt and about 5ml/1 tsp of the rice wine, egg white and cornflour paste.

2 Cut the broccoli heads into florets; remove the rough skin from the stalks, then slice the florets diagonally into diamond-shaped chunks.

3 Heat the oil in a preheated wok and stir-fry the prawns for about 30 seconds. Remove with a slotted spoon and drain thoroughly.

4 Pour off the excess oil, leaving 30ml/2 tbsp in the wok. Add the broccoli and spring onion, stir-fry for about 2 minutes, then add the remaining salt and the sugar, followed by the prawns and stock or water. Add the soy sauce and remaining rice wine or sherry. Blend well, then finally add the sesame oil and serve.

Curry Fried Pork and Rice Vermicelli Salad

Pork crackles add a delicious crunch to this popular salad.

INGREDIENTS

Serves 4

225g/8oz lean pork
2 garlic cloves, finely chopped
2 slices fresh root ginger,
    finely chopped
30−45ml/2−3 tbsp rice wine
45ml/3 tbsp vegetable oil
2 lemon grass stalks, finely chopped
10ml/2 tsp curry powder
175g/6oz beansprouts
225g/8oz rice vermicelli, soaked in
    warm water until soft
½ lettuce, finely shredded
30ml/2 tbsp mint leaves
lemon juice and fish sauce, to taste
salt and freshly ground black pepper
2 spring onions, chopped, 25g/1oz
    roasted peanuts, chopped, and pork
    crackles (optional), to garnish

1 Cut the pork into thin strips. Place in a shallow dish with half the garlic and ginger. Season with salt and pepper, pour over 30ml/2 tbsp rice wine and marinate for at least 1 hour.

2 Heat the oil in a frying pan. Add the remaining garlic and ginger and fry for a few seconds until fragrant. Stir in the pork, with the marinade, and add the lemon grass and curry powder. Fry until the pork is golden and cooked through, adding more rice wine if the mixture seems too dry.

3 Place the beansprouts in a sieve. Blanch them by lowering the sieve into a saucepan of boiling water for 1 minute, then drain and refresh under cold running water. Drain again. Using the same water, cook the drained rice vermicelli for 3−5 minutes until tender, drain and rinse under cold running water. Drain well and tip into a bowl.

4 Add the beansprouts, shredded lettuce and mint leaves to the rice vermicelli. Season with the lemon juice and fish sauce. Toss lightly.

5 Divide the noodle mixture among individual serving plates, making a nest on each plate. Arrange the pork mixture on top. Garnish with spring onions, roasted peanuts and pork crackles, if using.

Chilli Crabs

It is possible to find variations on *Kepiting Pedas* all over Asia. It will be memorable whether you eat in simple surroundings or in a sophisticated restaurant.

INGREDIENTS

Serves 4

2 cooked crabs, about 675g/1½lb
1cm/½in cube *terasi*
2 garlic cloves
2 fresh red chillies, seeded, or 5ml/
  1 tsp chopped chilli from a jar
1cm/½in fresh root ginger, peeled
  and sliced
60ml/4 tbsp sunflower oil
300ml/½ pint/1¼ cups tomato ketchup
15ml/1 tbsp dark brown sugar
150ml/¼ pint/⅔ cup warm water
4 spring onions, chopped, to garnish
cucumber chunks and hot toast,
  to serve (optional)

1 Remove the large claws of one crab and turn on to its back, with the head facing away from you. Use your thumbs to push the body up from the main shell. Discard the stomach sac and "dead men's fingers", i.e. lungs and any green matter. Leave the creamy brown meat in the shell and cut the shell in half, with a cleaver or strong knife. Cut the body section in half and crack the claws with a sharp blow from a hammer or cleaver. Avoid splintering the claws. Repeat with the other crab.

2 Grind the *terasi*, garlic, chillies and ginger to a paste in a food processor or with a pestle and mortar.

3 Heat a wok and add the oil. Fry the spice paste, stirring it all the time, without browning.

4 Stir in the tomato ketchup, sugar and water and mix the sauce well. When just boiling, add all the crab pieces and toss in the sauce until well-coated and hot. Serve in a large bowl, sprinkled with the spring onions. Place in the centre of the table for everyone to help themselves. Accompany this finger-licking dish with cool cucumber chunks and hot toast for mopping up the sauce, if you like.

Potato and Cellophane Noodle Salad

INGREDIENTS

Serves 4

2 medium potatoes, peeled and cut
  into eighths
175g/6oz cellophane noodles, soaked
  in hot water until soft
60ml/4 tbsp vegetable oil
1 onion, finely sliced
5ml/1 tsp ground turmeric
60ml/4 tbsp gram flour
5ml/1 tsp grated lemon rind
60–75ml/4–5 tbsp lemon juice
45ml/3 tbsp fish sauce
4 spring onions, finely sliced
salt and freshly ground black pepper

1 Place the potatoes in a saucepan.
Add water to cover, bring to the
boil and cook for about 15 minutes
until tender but firm. Drain the
potatoes and set them aside to cool.

2 Meanwhile, cook the drained
noodles in a saucepan of boiling
water for 3 minutes. Drain and rinse
under cold running water. Drain well.

3 Heat the oil in a frying pan. Add
the onion and turmeric and fry for
about 5 minutes until golden brown.
Drain the onion, reserving the oil.

4 Heat a small frying pan. Add the
gram flour and stir constantly for
about 4 minutes until it turns light
golden brown in colour.

5 Mix the potatoes, noodles and fried
onion in a large bowl. Add the
reserved oil and the toasted gram flour
with the lemon rind and juice, fish
sauce and spring onions. Mix together
well and adjust the seasoning to taste if
necessary. Serve at once.

Stir-fried Prawns with Tamarind

The sour, tangy flavour that is characteristic of many Thai dishes comes from tamarind. Fresh tamarind pods from the tamarind tree can sometimes be bought, but preparing them for cooking is a laborious process. The Thais, however, usually prefer to use compressed blocks of tamarind paste, which is simply soaked in warm water and then strained.

INGREDIENTS

Serves 4–6

50g/2oz tamarind paste
150ml/¼ pint/⅔ cup boiling water
30ml/2 tbsp vegetable oil
30ml/2 tbsp chopped onion
30ml/2 tbsp palm sugar
30ml/2 tbsp chicken stock or water
15ml/1 tbsp fish sauce
6 dried red chillies, fried
450g/1lb uncooked shelled prawns
15ml/1 tbsp fried chopped garlic
30ml/2 tbsp fried sliced shallots
2 spring onions, chopped, to garnish

1 Put the tamarind paste in a small bowl, pour over the boiling water and stir well to break up any lumps. Leave for 30 minutes. Strain, pushing as much of the juice through as possible. Measure 90ml/6 tbsp of the juice, the amount needed, and store the remainder in the fridge. Heat the oil in a wok. Add the chopped onion and fry until golden brown.

2 Add the sugar, stock, fish sauce, dried chillies and the tamarind juice, stirring well until the sugar dissolves. Bring to the boil.

3 Add the prawns, garlic and shallots. Stir-fry until the prawns are cooked, about 3–4 minutes. Garnish with the spring onions.

Egg Noodle Salad with Sesame Chicken

INGREDIENTS

Serves 4–6

400g/14oz fresh thin egg noodles
1 carrot, cut into long fine strips
50g/2oz mange-touts, topped, tailed,
  cut into fine strips and blanched
115g/4oz beansprouts, blanched
30ml/2 tbsp olive oil
225g/8oz skinless, boneless chicken
  breasts, finely sliced
30ml/2 tbsp sesame seeds, toasted
2 spring onions, finely sliced diagonally
  and coriander leaves, to garnish

For the dressing
45ml/3 tbsp sherry vinegar
75ml/5 tbsp soy sauce
60ml/4 tbsp sesame oil
90ml/6 tbsp light olive oil
1 garlic clove, finely chopped
5ml/1 tsp grated fresh root ginger
salt and freshly ground black pepper

1 To make the dressing. Combine all the ingredients in a small bowl with a pinch of salt and mix together well using a whisk or a fork.

2 Cook the noodles in a large saucepan of boiling water. Stir them occasionally to separate. They will only take a few minutes to cook: be careful not to overcook them. Drain, rinse under cold running water and drain well. Tip into a bowl.

3 Add the vegetables to the noodles. Pour in about half the dressing, then toss the mixture well and adjust the seasoning according to taste.

4 Heat the oil in a large frying pan. Add the chicken and stir-fry for 3 minutes, or until cooked and golden. Remove from the heat. Add the sesame seeds and drizzle in some of the remaining dressing.

5 Arrange the noodles on individual serving plates, making a nest on each plate. Spoon the chicken on top. Sprinkle with the sliced spring onions and the coriander leaves and serve any remaining dressing separately.

Satay Prawns

An enticing and tasty dish. Serve with greens and jasmine rice.

INGREDIENTS

Serves 4–6

450g/1lb king prawns, shelled, tail ends
  left intact and deveined
1/2 bunch coriander leaves, to garnish
4 red chillies, finely sliced, to garnish
spring onions, cut diagonally, to garnish

For the peanut sauce

45ml/3 tbsp vegetable oil
15ml/1 tbsp chopped garlic
1 small onion, chopped
3–4 red chillies, crushed and chopped
3 kaffir lime leaves, torn
1 stalk lemon grass, bruised
  and chopped
5ml/1 tsp medium curry paste
250ml/8fl oz/1 cup coconut milk
1.5cm/1/2in cinnamon stick
75g/3oz crunchy peanut butter
45ml/3 tbsp tamarind juice
30ml/2 tbsp fish sauce
30ml/2 tbsp palm sugar
juice of 1/2 lemon

1 To make the sauce, heat half the oil in a wok or large frying pan and add the garlic and onion. Cook until it softens, about 3–4 minutes.

2 Add the chillies, kaffir lime leaves, lemon grass and curry paste. Cook for a further 2–3 minutes.

COOK'S TIP

Curry paste has a far superior, authentic flavour to powdered varieties. Once opened, it should be kept in the fridge and used within 2 months.

---

3 Stir in the coconut milk, cinnamon stick, peanut butter, tamarind juice, fish sauce, palm sugar and lemon juice.

4 Reduce the heat and simmer gently for 15–20 minutes until the sauce thickens, stirring occasionally to ensure the sauce doesn't stick to the bottom of the wok or frying pan.

5 Heat the rest of the oil in a wok or large frying pan. Add the prawns and stir-fry for about 3–4 minutes or until the prawns turn pink and are slightly firm to the touch.

6 Mix the prawns with the sauce. Serve garnished with coriander leaves, red chillies and spring onions.

Cabbage Salad

A simple and delicious way of using cabbage. Other vegetables such as broccoli, cauliflower, beansprouts and Chinese cabbage can also be prepared this way.

INGREDIENTS

Serves 4–6

30ml/2 tbsp fish sauce
grated rind of 1 lime
30ml/2 tbsp lime juice
120ml/4fl oz/½ cup coconut milk
30ml/2 tbsp vegetable oil
2 large red chillies, seeded and finely
    cut into strips
6 garlic cloves, finely sliced
6 shallots, finely sliced
1 small cabbage, shredded
30ml/2 tbsp coarsely chopped roasted
    peanuts, to serve

1 Make the dressing by combining the fish sauce, lime rind and juice and coconut milk. Set aside.

2 Heat the oil in a wok or frying pan. Stir-fry the chillies, garlic and shallots, until the shallots are brown and crisp. Remove and set aside.

3 Blanch the cabbage in boiling salted water for about 2–3 minutes, drain and put into a bowl.

4 Stir the dressing into the cabbage, toss and mix well. Transfer the salad into a serving dish. Sprinkle with the fried shallot mixture and the chopped roasted peanuts.

Spiced Prawns with Coconut

This spicy dish is based on the traditional Indonesian dish *Sambal Goreng Udang*. Sambals are pungent, very hot dishes popular throughout south India and South-east Asia.

INGREDIENTS

Serves 3–4

2–3 red chillies, seeded and chopped
3 shallots, chopped
1 lemon grass stalk, chopped
2 garlic cloves, chopped
thin sliver of dried shrimp paste
2.5ml/½ tsp ground galangal
5ml/1 tsp ground turmeric
5ml/1 tsp ground coriander
15ml/1 tbsp groundnut oil
250ml/8fl oz/1 cup water
2 fresh kaffir lime leaves
5ml/1 tsp light brown soft sugar
2 tomatoes, skinned, seeded and chopped
250ml/8fl oz/1 cup coconut milk
675g/1½lb large raw prawns, peeled and deveined
squeeze of lemon juice
salt
shredded spring onions and flaked coconut, to garnish

1 In a mortar, pound together the chillies, shallots, lemon grass, garlic, shrimp paste, galangal, turmeric and coriander with a pestle until the mixture forms a paste.

2 Heat a wok, add the oil and swirl it around. Add the spice paste and stir-fry for 2 minutes. Pour in the water and add the kaffir lime leaves, sugar and tomatoes. Simmer for 8–10 minutes until most of the liquid has evaporated.

--- COOK'S TIP ---

Dried shrimp paste, widely used in South-east Asian cooking, is available from oriental food stores. Ground galangal, which is similar to ground ginger and comes from the same family, is also available from oriental food stores.

3 Add the coconut milk and prawns and cook gently, stirring, for 4 minutes until the prawns are pink. Season with lemon juice and salt to taste. Transfer the mixture to a warmed serving dish, garnish with the spring onions and flaked coconut and serve.

Thai Seafood Salad

This seafood salad with chilli, lemon grass and fish sauce is light and refreshing.

INGREDIENTS

Serves 4
225g/8oz ready-prepared squid
225g/8oz raw tiger prawns
8 scallops, shelled
225g/8oz firm white fish
30–45ml/2–3 tbsp olive oil
small mixed lettuce leaves and
    coriander sprigs, to serve

For the dressing
2 small fresh red chillies, seeded and
    finely chopped
5cm/2in lemon grass stalk,
    finely chopped
2 fresh kaffir lime leaves, shredded
30ml/2 tbsp Thai fish sauce (*nam pla*)
2 shallots, thinly sliced
30ml/2 tbsp lime juice
30ml/2 tbsp rice vinegar
10ml/2 tsp caster sugar

1 Prepare the seafood: slit open the squid bodies. Score the flesh with a sharp knife, then cut into square pieces. Halve the tentacles, if necessary. Peel and devein the prawns. Remove the dark beard-like fringe and tough muscle from the scallops. Cube the white fish.

COOK'S TIP

It is important to ensure that the prawns are cooked properly as undercooked prawns can carry infection.

2 Heat a wok until hot. Add the oil and swirl it around, then add the prawns and stir-fry for 2–3 minutes until pink. Transfer to a large bowl. Stir-fry the squid and scallops for 1–2 minutes until opaque. Remove and add to the prawns. Stir-fry the white fish for 2–3 minutes. Remove and add to the cooked seafood. Reserve any juices.

3 Put all the dressing ingredients in a small bowl with the reserved juices from the wok; mix well.

4 Pour the dressing over the seafood and toss gently. Arrange the salad leaves and coriander sprigs on four individual plates, then spoon the seafood on top. Serve at once.

Oriental Scallops with Ginger Relish

Buy scallops in their shells to be absolutely sure of their freshness; your fishmonger will open them for you if you find this difficult. Remember to ask for the shells, which make excellent and attractive serving dishes. Queen scallops are particularly prized for their delicate-tasting coral or roe.

INGREDIENTS

Serves 4
8 king or queen scallops
4 whole star anise
25g/1oz unsalted butter
salt and ground white pepper
fresh chervil sprigs and whole star
   anise, to garnish

For the relish
¹/₂ cucumber, peeled
salt, for sprinkling
5cm/2in fresh root ginger, peeled
10ml/2 tsp caster sugar
45ml/3 tbsp rice wine vinegar
10ml/2 tsp ginger juice, strained from
   a jar of stem ginger
sesame seeds, to garnish

1 To make the relish, halve the cucumber lengthways and scoop out the seeds with a teaspoon and discard.

2 Cut the cucumber into 2.5cm/1in pieces, place in a colander and sprinkle liberally with salt. Set aside for 30 minutes.

3 Open the scallop shells, detach the scallops and remove the edible parts. Cut each scallop into two or three slices and reserve the corals. Coarsely grind the star anise in a mortar with a pestle.

4 Place the scallop slices and corals in a bowl, sprinkle over the star anise and season with salt and pepper. Set aside to marinate for about 1 hour.

5 Rinse the cucumber under cold water, drain well and pat dry on kitchen paper. Cut the ginger into thin julienne strips and mix with the cucumber, sugar, vinegar and ginger juice. Cover and chill until needed.

6 Heat a wok and add the butter. Add the scallop slices and corals and stir-fry for 2–3 minutes. Garnish with sprigs of chervil and whole star anise, and serve with the cucumber relish, sprinkled with sesame seeds.

--- COOK'S TIP ---

To prepare scallops, hold the shell, flat side up, and insert a strong knife between the shells to cut through the muscle. Separate the two shells. Slide the knife blade underneath the scallop in the bottom shell to cut the second muscle. Remove the scallop and separate the edible parts – the white muscle and orange coral or roe. The skirt can be used for making fish stock, but the other parts should be discarded.

Vegetable Salad with Hot Peanut Sauce

A wok is ideal for dry-frying as well as stir-frying, and here it is used to great effect in making this wonderful peanut sauce.

INGREDIENTS

Serves 4–6

2 potatoes, peeled
175g/6oz French beans, topped
  and tailed

For the peanut sauce
150g/5oz peanuts
15ml/1 tbsp vegetable oil
2 shallots or 1 small onion,
  finely chopped
1 clove garlic, crushed
1–2 small chillies, seeded and
  finely chopped
1cm/½ in square shrimp paste, or
  15ml/1 tbsp fish sauce (optional)
30ml/2 tbsp tamarind sauce
100ml/4fl oz/½ cup canned
  coconut milk
15ml/1 tbsp clear honey

For the salad
175g/6oz Chinese leaves, shredded
1 iceberg or bib lettuce, separated
  into leaves
175g/6oz beansprouts, washed
½ cucumber, cut into fingers
150g/5oz giant white radish, shredded
3 spring onions, trimmed
225g/8oz tofu, cut into large dice
3 hard-boiled eggs, quartered

1 Bring the potatoes to the boil in salted water and simmer for 20 minutes. Cook the beans for 3–4 minutes. Drain the potatoes and beans and refresh under cold running water.

2 For the peanut sauce, dry-fry the peanuts in a wok, or place under a moderate grill, tossing them all the time to prevent burning. Turn the peanuts on to a clean dish cloth and rub vigorously to remove the papery skins. Place the peanuts in a food processor or blender and process for 2 minutes.

3 Heat the vegetable oil in a wok and soften the shallots or onion, garlic and chillies without letting them colour. Add the shrimp paste or fish sauce if using, together with the tamarind sauce, coconut milk and honey. Simmer briefly, add to the peanuts and process in a food processor to form a thick sauce.

4 Arrange the salad ingredients, potatoes and beans on a large platter and serve with a bowl of the peanut sauce.

MEAT

Pork, beef and lamb are all superb when stir-fried, but using tender cuts and making sure the meat is cut into even-sized strips or cubes are the keys to success. Most of the recipes here include a delicious selection of vegetables cooked together with the meat in the same wok, so the only extras you need to prepare are some rice, a salad or, perhaps, freshly baked naan. Recipes range from the exotic stir-fried pork with lychees to the hot and spicy chilli beef with basil and from the delicately flavoured glazed lamb to melt-in-the-mouth oriental beef.

Bean Curd and Cucumber Salad

Tahu Goreng Ketjap is a nutritious and refreshing salad with a hot, sweet and sour dressing. It is ideal for buffets.

INGREDIENTS

Serves 4–6
1 small cucumber
oil for frying
1 square fresh or 115g/4oz long-life
   bean curd
115g/4oz beansprouts, trimmed
   and rinsed
salt

For the dressing
1 small onion, grated
2 garlic cloves, crushed
2.5ml/½ tsp chilli powder
30–45ml/2–3 tbsp dark soy sauce
15–30ml/1–2 tbsp rice-wine vinegar
10ml/2 tsp dark brown sugar
salt
celery leaves, to garnish

1 Trim the ends from the cucumber and then cut it in neat cubes. Sprinkle with salt and set aside, while preparing the remaining ingredients.

2 Cut the bean curd into cubes. Heat a little oil in a pan and fry the bean curd on all sides until golden brown. Drain on absorbent kitchen paper.

COOK'S TIP

Beansprouts come from the mung bean and are easily grown at home on damp cotton or in a plastic bean sprouter. They must be eaten when absolutely fresh, so when buying from a shop check that they are crisp and are not beginning to go brown or soft. Eat within a day or two.

3 Prepare the dressing by blending together the onion, garlic and chilli powder. Stir in the soy sauce, vinegar, sugar and salt to taste. You can do this in a screw-topped glass jar.

4 Just before serving, rinse the cucumber under cold running water. Drain and dry thoroughly. Toss the cucumber, bean curd and beansprouts together in a serving bowl and pour over the dressing. Garnish with the celery leaves and serve the salad at once.

Lemon Grass Pork

Chillies and lemon grass flavour this simple stir-fry, while peanuts add crunch.

INGREDIENTS

Serves 4

675g/1½lb boneless loin of pork
2 lemon grass stalks, finely chopped
4 spring onions, thinly sliced
5ml/1 tsp salt
12 black peppercorns, coarsely crushed
30ml/2 tbsp groundnut oil
2 garlic cloves, chopped
2 fresh red chillies, seeded and chopped
5ml/1 tsp light brown soft sugar
30ml/2 tbsp Thai fish sauce (*nam pla*), or to taste
25g/1oz roasted unsalted peanuts, chopped
salt and ground black pepper
coriander leaves, to garnish
rice noodles, to serve

1 Trim any excess fat from the pork. Cut the meat across into 5mm/¼in thick slices, then cut each slice into 5mm/¼in strips. Put the pork into a bowl with the lemon grass, spring onions, salt and crushed peppercorns. Mix well, then cover and leave to marinate for 30 minutes.

2 Heat a wok until hot, add the oil and swirl it around. Add the pork mixture and stir-fry for 3 minutes.

3 Add the garlic and chillies and stir-fry for a further 5–8 minutes over a medium heat until the pork no longer looks pink.

4 Add the sugar, fish sauce and chopped peanuts and toss to mix. Taste and adjust the seasoning, if necessary. Serve at once, garnished with roughly torn coriander leaves on a bed of rice noodles.

SALADS

Stir-frying is a good way of creating some interesting and unusual salads, as flavours can be blended without any loss of the all-important crispness and texture. Vegetables, seafood, chicken and noodles are just some of the ingredients that can be combined to make delicious summer meals or refreshing side dishes to serve at any time of year. Try the tantalizing vegetable salad with a hot peanut sauce, the mouth-watering combination of chicken and spices in a Thai salad or the marvellous, crunchy curry fried pork and rice vermicelli salad.

Stir-fried Pork with Lychees

Crispy pieces of pork with fleshy lychees make an unusual stir-fry that is ideal for a dinner party.

INGREDIENTS

Serves 4

450g/1lb fatty pork, such as belly pork
30ml/2 tbsp hoi-sin sauce
4 spring onions, sliced
175g/6oz lychees, peeled, stoned and
  cut into slivers
salt and ground black pepper
fresh lychees and fresh parsley sprigs,
  to garnish

1 Cut the pork into bitesize pieces.

2 Pour the hoi-sin sauce over the pork and marinate for 30 minutes.

COOK'S TIP

If you cannot buy fresh lychees, this dish can be made with drained canned lychees.

3 Heat the wok, then add the pork and stir-fry for 5 minutes until crisp and golden. Add the spring onions and stir-fry for a further 2 minutes.

4 Scatter the lychee slivers over the pork, and season well with salt and pepper. Garnish with fresh lychees and parsley, and serve.

Deep-fried Onions

Known as *Bawang Goreng*, these are a traditional accompaniment and garnish to many Indonesian dishes. Oriental stores sell them ready-prepared, but it is simple to make them at home, using fresh onions. The small red onions that may be bought in Asian food stores are excellent when deep-fried as they contain less water than most European varieties.

INGREDIENTS

Makes 450g / 1lb
450g/1lb onions
oil for deep-frying

1 Peel and slice the onions as evenly and finely as possible.

2 Spread out thinly on kitchen paper in an airy place and leave to dry for 30 minutes–2 hours.

3 Heat the oil in a wok to 190°C/ 375°F. Fry the onions in batches, turning all the time, until they are crisp and golden. Drain well on kitchen paper and cool. Deep-fried onions can be stored in an airtight container.

COOK'S TIP

Garlic can also be prepared and cooked in the same way or some can be fried with the last batch of onions. Deep-fried garlic gives an added dimension in flavour as a garnish for many dishes.

An even faster way to prepare home-made deep-fried onions is to use a 75g/3oz packet of quick-dried onions, which you can fry in about 250ml/8fl oz/1 cup sunflower oil. This gives you 115g/4oz of fried onion flakes.

Savoury Pork Ribs with Snake Beans

This is a rich and pungent dish. If snake beans are hard to find, you can substitute fine green or runner beans.

INGREDIENTS

Serves 4–6

675g/1½lb pork spare ribs or belly of pork
30ml/2 tbsp vegetable oil
120ml/4fl oz/½ cup water
15ml/1 tbsp palm sugar
15ml/1 tbsp fish sauce
150g/5oz snake beans, cut into 5cm/2in lengths
2 kaffir lime leaves, finely sliced
2 red chillies, finely sliced, to garnish

For the chilli paste

3 dried red chillies, seeded and soaked
4 shallots, chopped
4 garlic cloves, chopped
5ml/1 tsp chopped galangal
1 stalk lemon grass, chopped
6 black peppercorns
5ml/1 tsp shrimp paste
30ml/2 tbsp dried shrimp, rinsed

1 Put all the ingredients for the chilli paste in a mortar and grind together with a pestle until it forms a thick paste.

2 Slice and chop the spare ribs (or belly pork) into 4cm/1½in lengths.

3 Heat the oil in a wok or frying pan. Add the pork and fry for about 5 minutes, until lightly browned.

4 Stir in the chilli paste and continue to cook for another 5 minutes, stirring constantly to stop the paste from sticking to the pan.

5 Add the water, cover and simmer for 7–10 minutes or until the spare ribs are tender. Season with palm sugar and fish sauce.

6 Mix in the snake beans and kaffir lime leaves and fry until the beans are cooked. Serve garnished with sliced red chillies.

Broccoli in Oyster Sauce

The broccoli florets retain their vivid shade of green and crunchy texture, as well as much of their vitamin and mineral content, when given the wok treatment here. Vegetarians may prefer to substitute light soy sauce for the oyster sauce.

INGREDIENTS

Serves 4

450g/1lb broccoli
45–60ml/3–4 tbsp vegetable oil
2.5ml/½ tsp salt
2.5ml/½ tsp light brown sugar
30–45ml/2–3 tbsp stock or water
30ml/2 tbsp oyster sauce

1 Cut the broccoli heads into florets, remove the rough skin from the stalks and slice the florets diagonally into diamond-shaped chunks.

2 Heat the oil in a preheated wok and add the salt, then stir-fry the broccoli for about 2 minutes. Add the sugar and stock or water, and continue stirring for 1 minute. Finally add the oyster sauce, blend well and serve.

— COOK'S TIP —

Always choose healthy-looking broccoli with firm stems that are neither woody nor wrinkled. Look for tightly packed, well-coloured flower heads with no signs of yellowing. Broccoli is best eaten on the day it was purchased or, better still, picked. It deteriorates rapidly in storage and loses many of the vitamins for which it is especially valued, as well as its crispness.

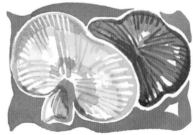

Spicy Meatballs

Serve *Pergedel Djawa* with either a *sambal* or spicy sauce.

INGREDIENTS

Makes 24

1 large onion, roughly chopped
1–2 fresh red chillies, seeded and chopped
2 garlic cloves, crushed
1cm/½in cube *terasi*, prepared
15ml/1 tbsp coriander seeds
5ml/1 tsp cumin seeds
450g/1lb lean minced beef
10ml/2 tsp dark soy sauce
5ml/1 tsp dark brown sugar
juice of ½ lemon
a little beaten egg
oil for shallow-frying
salt and freshly ground black pepper
fresh coriander sprigs, to garnish

1 Put the onion, chillies, garlic and *terasi* in a food processor. Process but do not over-chop or the onion will become too wet and spoil the consistency of the meatballs. Dry-fry the coriander and cumin seeds in a preheated pan for about 1 minute, to release the aroma. Do not brown. Grind with a pestle and mortar.

2 Put the meat in a large bowl. Stir in the onion mixture. Add the ground coriander and cumin, soy sauce, seasoning, sugar and lemon juice. Bind with a little beaten egg and shape into small, even-size balls.

3 Chill the meatballs briefly to firm up, if necessary. Fry in shallow oil, turning often, until cooked through and browned. This will take 4–5 minutes, depending on their size.

4 Remove from the pan, drain well on kitchen paper and serve, garnished with coriander sprigs.

Pak Choi and Mushroom Stir-fry

Try to buy all the varieties of mushroom for this dish – wild oyster and shiitake mushrooms have particularly distinctive, delicate flavours that work well when stir-fried.

INGREDIENTS

Serves 4

4 dried black Chinese mushrooms
150ml/¼ pint/⅔ cup hot water
450g/1lb pak choi
50g/2oz oyster mushrooms,
  preferably wild
50g/2oz shiitake mushrooms
15ml/1 tbsp vegetable oil
1 clove garlic, crushed
30ml/2 tbsp oyster sauce

1 Soak the black Chinese mushrooms in the hot water for 15 minutes to soften.

2 Tear the pak choi into bitesize pieces with your fingers.

3 Halve any large oyster and shiitake mushrooms, using a sharp knife.

4 Strain the Chinese mushrooms. Heat the wok, then add the oil. When the oil is hot, stir-fry the garlic until softened but not coloured.

5 Add the pak choi to the wok and stir-fry for 1 minute. Mix in all the mushrooms and stir-fry for 1 minute.

6 Add the oyster sauce, toss well and serve immediately.

> ── COOK'S TIP ──
>
> Pak choi, also called bok choi, pok choi and spoon cabbage, is an attractive member of the cabbage family, with long, smooth white stems and dark green leaves. It has a pleasant flavour which does not, in any way, resemble that of cabbage.

Oriental Beef

This sumptuous stir-fried beef melts in the mouth, and is perfectly complemented by the delicious crunchy relish.

INGREDIENTS

Serves 4
450g/1lb rump steak
15ml/1 tbsp sunflower oil
4 whole radishes, to garnish

For the marinade
2 cloves garlic, crushed
60ml/4 tbsp dark soy sauce
30ml/2 tbsp dry sherry
10ml/2 tsp soft dark brown sugar

For the relish
6 radishes
10cm/4in piece cucumber
1 piece stem ginger

1 Cut the beef into thin strips. Place in a bowl.

2 To make the marinade, mix together the garlic, soy sauce, sherry and sugar in a bowl. Pour it over the beef and leave to marinate overnight.

COOK'S TIP

Dark soy sauce has a stronger, more robust flavour than light soy sauce. It is particularly useful for imparting a rich, dark colour to meat dishes.

3 To make the relish, chop the radishes and cucumber into short matchsticks, then cut the ginger into small matchsticks. Mix thoroughly together in a bowl.

4 Heat a wok, then add the oil. When the oil is hot, add the meat and the marinade and stir-fry for 3–4 minutes. Serve with the relish, and garnish with a whole radish on each plate.

Spicy Courgette Fritters with Thai Salsa

The Thai salsa goes just as well with plain stir-fried salmon strips or stir-fried beef as it does with these courgette fritters.

INGREDIENTS

Serves 2–4

10ml/2 tsp cumin seeds
10ml/2 tsp coriander seeds
450g/1lb courgettes
115g/4oz chick-pea (gram) flour
2.5ml/½ tsp bicarbonate of soda
120ml/4fl oz/½ cup groundnut oil
salt and ground black pepper
fresh mint sprigs, to garnish

For the Thai salsa

½ cucumber, diced
3 spring onions, chopped
6 radishes, cubed
30ml/2 tbsp fresh mint, chopped
2.5cm/1in fresh root ginger, peeled
  and grated
45ml/3 tbsp lime juice
30ml/2 tbsp caster sugar
3 cloves garlic, crushed

1 Heat the wok, then dry-fry the cumin and coriander seeds. Cool them, then grind well, using a pestle and mortar.

COOK'S TIP

You can substitute mooli, also known as daikon and white radish, for the round radishes in the salsa.

2 Cut the courgettes into 7.5cm/3in sticks. Place in a bowl.

3 Process the flour, bicarbonate of soda, spices and salt and pepper in a food processor or blender. Add 120ml/4fl oz warm water with 15ml/1 tbsp groundnut oil and process again.

4 Coat the courgettes in the batter, then leave to stand for 10 minutes.

5 To make the salsa, mix together the cucumber, spring onions, radishes, mint, ginger and lime juice in a bowl. Stir in the sugar and the garlic.

6 Heat the wok, then add the remaining oil. When the oil is hot, stir-fry the courgettes in batches. Drain well on kitchen paper, then serve hot with the Thai salsa, garnished with fresh mint sprigs.

Pork with Eggs and Mushrooms

Traditionally, this stir-fried dish is served as a filling wrapped in thin pancakes, but it can also be served on its own with plain rice.

INGREDIENTS

Serves 4

15g/½ oz dried Chinese mushrooms
175–225g/6–8oz pork fillet
225g/8oz Chinese leaves
115g/4oz bamboo shoots, drained
2 spring onions
3 eggs
5ml/1 tsp salt
60ml/4 tbsp vegetable oil
15ml/1 tbsp light soy sauce
15ml/1 tbsp Chinese rice wine or
  dry sherry
few drops sesame oil

1 Rinse the mushrooms thoroughly in cold water and then soak in warm water for 25–30 minutes. Rinse thoroughly again and discard the hard stalks, if there are any. Dry the mushrooms and thinly shred.

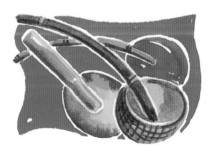

2 Cut the pork fillet into matchstick-size shreds. Thinly shred the Chinese leaves, bamboo shoots and spring onions.

3 Heat the remaining oil in the wok and stir-fry the pork for about 1 minute, or until the colour changes.

4 Beat the eggs with a pinch of salt. Heat a little oil in a wok, add the eggs and lightly scramble, but do not make too dry. Remove from the wok.

5 Add the vegetables to the wok and stir-fry for 1 minute.

6 Add the remaining salt, the soy sauce and rice wine or sherry. Stir for 1 further minute before adding the scrambled eggs. Break up the scrambled eggs and blend well. Sprinkle with sesame oil and serve.

Cooked Vegetable Gado-Gado

Instead of putting everything on a large platter, you can serve individual servings of this salad. It is a perfect recipe for lunchtime or informal gatherings.

INGREDIENTS

Serves 6

225g/8oz waxy potatoes, cooked
450g/1lb mixed cabbage, spinach and beansprouts, in equal proportions, rinsed and shredded
½ cucumber, cut in wedges, salted and set aside for 15 minutes
2–3 eggs, hard-boiled and shelled
115g/4oz fresh bean curd
oil for frying
6–8 large prawn crackers
lemon juice
Deep-fried Onions, to garnish
Peanut Sauce, see Vegetable Salad with Hot Peanut Sauce

1 Cube the potatoes and set aside. Bring a large pan of salted water to the boil. Plunge one type of raw vegetable at a time into the pan for just a few seconds to blanch. Lift out the vegetables with a large draining spoon or sieve and run under very cold water. Or plunge them into iced water and leave for 2 minutes. Drain thoroughly. Blanch all the vegetables, except the cucumber, in this way.

2 Rinse the cucumber pieces and drain them well. Cut the eggs in quarters. Cut the bean curd into cubes.

3 Fry the bean curd in hot oil in a wok until crisp on both sides. Lift out and drain on kitchen paper.

4 Add more oil to the pan and then deep-fry the Prawn Crackers one or two at a time. Reserve them on a tray lined with kitchen paper.

5 Arrange all the cooked vegetables attractively on a platter, with the cucumber, hard-boiled eggs and bean curd. Scatter with the lemon juice and Deep-fried Onions at the last minute.

6 Serve with the prepared Peanut Sauce and hand round the fried prawn crackers separately.

Chilli Beef with Basil

This is a dish for chilli lovers! It is very easy to prepare – all you need is a wok.

INGREDIENTS

Serves 2

about 90ml/6 tbsp groundnut oil
16–20 large fresh basil leaves
275g/10oz rump steak
30ml/2 tbsp Thai fish sauce (*nam pla*)
5ml/1 tsp dark brown soft sugar
1–2 fresh red chillies, sliced into rings
3 garlic cloves, chopped
5ml/1 tsp chopped fresh root ginger
1 shallot, thinly sliced
30ml/2 tbsp finely chopped fresh basil leaves, plus extra to garnish
squeeze of lemon juice
salt and ground black pepper
Thai jasmine rice, to serve

1 Heat the oil in a wok and, when hot, add the whole basil leaves and fry for about 1 minute until crisp and golden. Drain on kitchen paper. Remove the wok from the heat and pour off all but 30ml/2 tbsp of the oil.

COOK'S TIP

Although not so familiar to western cooks, Thai fish sauce is as widely used in Thai cooking as soy sauce is in Chinese cuisine. In fact, they are not dissimilar in appearance and taste. Called *nam pla*, Thai fish sauce is available at oriental food stores, but if you cannot get it, soy sauce is an adequate substitute.

2 Cut the steak across the grain into thin strips. Mix together the fish sauce and sugar in a bowl. Add the beef, mix well, then leave to marinate for about 30 minutes.

3 Reheat the oil until hot, add the chilli, garlic, ginger and shallot and stir-fry for 30 seconds. Add the beef and chopped basil, then stir-fry for about 3 minutes. Flavour with lemon juice and salt and pepper to taste.

4 Transfer to a warmed serving plate, scatter over the basil leaves to garnish and serve immediately with Thai jasmine rice.

Tofu Stir-fry

The tofu has a pleasant creamy texture, which contrasts delightfully with the crunchy stir-fried vegetables. Make sure you buy firm tofu which is easy to cut neatly.

INGREDIENTS

Serves 2–4

115g/4oz hard white cabbage
2 green chillies
225g/8oz firm tofu
45ml/3 tbsp vegetable oil
2 cloves garlic, crushed
3 spring onions, chopped
175g/6oz French beans, topped
  and tailed
175g/6oz baby sweetcorn, halved
115g/4oz beansprouts
45ml/3 tbsp smooth peanut butter
25ml/1½ tbsp dark soy sauce
300ml/½ pint/1¼ cups coconut milk

2 Heat the wok, then add 30ml/ 2 tbsp of the oil. When the oil is hot, add the tofu, stir-fry for 3 minutes and remove. Set aside. Wipe out the wok with kitchen paper.

3 Add the remaining oil. When it is hot, add the garlic, spring onions and chillies and stir-fry for 1 minute. Add the French beans, sweetcorn and beansprouts and stir-fry for a further 2 minutes.

4 Add the peanut butter and soy sauce to the wok. Stir well to coat the vegetables. Add the tofu to the vegetables in the wok.

5 Pour the coconut milk over the vegetables, simmer for 3 minutes and serve immediately.

1 Shred the white cabbage. Carefully remove the seeds from the chillies and chop finely. Wear rubber gloves to protect your hands, if necessary. Cut the tofu into strips.

Thai Sweet and Sour Pork

Sweet and sour is traditionally a Chinese creation but the Thais do it very well. This version has an altogether fresher and cleaner flavour and it makes a good one-dish meal when served over rice.

INGREDIENTS

Serves 4

350g/12oz lean pork
30ml/2 tbsp vegetable oil
4 garlic cloves, finely sliced
1 small red onion, sliced
30ml/2 tbsp fish sauce
15ml/1 tbsp granulated sugar
1 red pepper, seeded and diced
½ cucumber, seeded and sliced
2 plum tomatoes, cut into wedges
115g/4oz pineapple, cut into
  small chunks
freshly ground black pepper
2 spring onions, cut into short lengths
coriander leaves, to garnish
spring onions, shredded, to garnish

1 Slice the pork into thin strips. Heat the oil in a wok or large frying pan.

2 Add the garlic and fry until golden, then add the pork and stir-fry for about 4–5 minutes. Add the onion.

3 Season with fish sauce, sugar and freshly ground black pepper. Stir and cook for 3–4 minutes, or until the pork is cooked.

4 Add the rest of the vegetables, the pineapple and spring onions. You may need to add a few tablespoons of water. Continue to stir-fry for another 3–4 minutes. Serve hot, garnished with coriander leaves and spring onion.

Chinese Leaves with Oyster Sauce

Here, Chinese leaves are prepared in a very simple way – stir-fried and served with oyster sauce. This Cantonese combination makes a simple, quickly prepared and tasty accompaniment to oriental or western seafood dishes. Vegetarians may prefer to substitute light soy or hoi-sin sauce for the oyster sauce used in this recipe.

INGREDIENTS

Serves 3–4
450g/1lb Chinese leaves
30ml/2 tbsp groundnut oil
15–30ml/1–2 tbsp oyster sauce

1 Trim the Chinese leaves, removing any discoloured leaves and damaged stems. Tear into manageable pieces.

2 Heat a wok until hot, add the oil and swirl it around.

3 Add the Chinese leaves and stir-fry for 2–3 minutes until they have wilted a little.

4 Add the oyster sauce and continue to stir-fry for a few seconds more until the leaves are cooked but still slightly crisp. Serve immediately.

COOK'S TIP

You can replace the Chinese leaves with Chinese flowering cabbage, which is also known by its Cantonese name *choi sam*. It has bright green leaves and tiny yellow flowers, which are also eaten along with the leaves and stalks. It is available from oriental supermarkets.

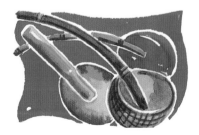

Sizzling Beef with Celeriac Straw

The crisp celeriac matchsticks look like fine pieces of straw when stir-fried, and they have a mild celery-like flavour that is quite delicious.

INGREDIENTS

Serves 4

450g/1lb celeriac
150ml/¼ pint/⅔ cup vegetable oil
1 red pepper
6 spring onions
450g/1lb rump steak
60ml/4 tbsp beef stock
30ml/2 tbsp sherry vinegar
10ml/2 tsp Worcestershire sauce
10ml/2 tsp tomato purée
salt and ground black pepper

1 Peel the celeriac and then cut into fine matchsticks, using a cleaver.

2 Heat a wok, then add two-thirds of the oil. When the oil is hot, fry the celeriac matchsticks in batches until golden brown and crispy. Drain well on kitchen paper.

3 Halve, core and seed the red pepper, then slice diagonally into 2.5cm/1in lengths. Slice the spring onions diagonally into 2.5cm/ 1in lengths.

4 Chop the beef into thin strips, across the grain of the meat.

5 Heat the wok again and add the remaining oil. When the oil is hot, stir-fry the chopped red pepper and spring onion for 2–3 minutes.

6 Add the beef strips and stir-fry for a further 3–4 minutes until browned. Add the stock, vinegar, Worcestershire sauce and tomato purée. Season to taste and serve with the celeriac straw.

--- COOK'S TIP ---

Avoid buying very large celeriac roots, as they tend to be woody or otherwise unpleasant in texture. As it is rather an unwieldy and knobbly vegetable, celeriac is easier to peel properly if you cut it into more or less even-sized slices first. Then peel each slice individually using a very sharp knife. They need to be peeled quite thickly to obtain a neat edge. You can then easily cut the slices into thin strips.

Stir-fried Spinach with Garlic and Sesame Seeds

The sesame seeds add a crunchy texture that contrasts well with the wilted spinach in this easy vegetable dish.

INGREDIENTS

Serves 2

225g/8oz fresh spinach, washed
25ml/1½ tbsp sesame seeds
30ml/2 tbsp groundnut oil
1.5ml/¼ tsp sea salt flakes
2–3 garlic cloves, sliced

— COOK'S TIP —

Take care when adding the spinach to the hot oil as it will spit furiously.

1 Shake the spinach to get rid of any excess water, then remove the stalks and discard any yellow or damaged leaves. Lay several spinach leaves one on top of another, roll up tightly and cut crossways into wide strips. Repeat with the remaining leaves.

2 Heat a wok to a medium heat, add the sesame seeds and dry-fry, stirring constantly, for 1–2 minutes until golden brown. Transfer to a small bowl and set aside.

3 Add the oil to the wok and swirl it around. When hot, add the salt, spinach and garlic and stir-fry for 2 minutes until the spinach just wilts and the leaves are coated in oil.

4 Sprinkle over the dry-fried sesame seeds and toss well. Serve at once.

Stir-fried Beef in Oyster Sauce

Another simple but delicious recipe. In Thailand fresh straw mushrooms are readily available, but oyster mushrooms make a good substitute. To make the dish even more interesting, use several types of mushroom.

INGREDIENTS

Serves 4–6

450g/1lb rump steak
30ml/2 tbsp soy sauce
15ml/1 tbsp cornflour
45ml/3 tbsp vegetable oil
15ml/1 tbsp chopped garlic
15ml/1 tbsp chopped root ginger
225g/8oz mixed mushrooms such as shiitake, oyster and straw
30ml/2 tbsp oyster sauce
5ml/1 tsp granulated sugar
4 spring onions, cut into short lengths
freshly ground black pepper
2 red chillies, cut into strips, to garnish

1 Slice the beef, on the diagonal, into long thin strips. Mix together the soy sauce and cornflour in a large bowl, stir in the beef and leave to marinate for 1–2 hours.

— COOK'S TIP —

Made from extracts of oysters, oyster sauce is velvety smooth and has a savoury sweet and meaty taste. There are several types available; buy the best you can afford.

2 Heat half the oil in a wok or frying pan. Add the garlic and ginger and fry until fragrant. Stir in the beef. Stir to separate the strips, let them colour and cook for 1–2 minutes. Remove from the pan and set aside.

3 Heat the remaining oil in the wok. Add the shiitake, oyster and straw mushrooms. Cook until tender.

4 Return the beef to the wok with the mushrooms. Add the oyster sauce, sugar and freshly ground black pepper to taste. Mix well.

5 Add the spring onions. Mix together. Serve garnished with strips of red chilli.

Black Bean and Vegetable Stir-fry

The secret of a quick stir-fry is proper preparation of all the ingredients first. It is important that the ingredients are added to the wok in the right order so that the larger or thicker pieces have a longer cooking time than the smaller pieces – even if this is a difference of only a few millimetres and a few seconds!

INGREDIENTS

Serves 4
8 spring onions
225g/8oz button mushrooms
1 red pepper
1 green pepper
2 large carrots
60ml/4 tbsp sesame oil
2 garlic cloves, crushed
60ml/4 tbsp black bean sauce
90ml/6 tbsp warm water
225g/8oz beansprouts
salt and ground black pepper

2 Cut both the peppers in half, remove the seeds and slice the flesh into thin strips.

3 Cut the carrots in half. Cut each half into thin strips lengthways. Stack the slices and cut through them to make very fine strips.

4 Heat the oil in a large preheated wok until very hot. Add the spring onions and garlic and stir-fry for 30 seconds.

5 Add the mushrooms, peppers and carrots. Stir-fry for 5–6 minutes over a high heat until the vegetables are just beginning to soften.

6 Mix the black bean sauce with the water. Add to the wok and cook for 3–4 minutes. Stir in the beansprouts and cook for 1 minute more, until all the vegetables are coated in the sauce. Season to taste, then serve at once.

1 Thinly slice the spring onions and button mushrooms.

Dry-fried Shredded Beef

Dry-frying is a unique Szechuan cooking method, in which the main ingredient is firstly stir-fried slowly over a low heat until dry, then finished off quickly with a mixture of other ingredients over a high heat.

INGREDIENTS

Serves 4

350–400g/12–14oz beef steak
1 large or 2 small carrots
2–3 sticks celery
30ml/2 tbsp sesame oil
15ml/1 tbsp Chinese rice wine or
  dry sherry
15ml/1 tbsp chilli bean sauce
15ml/1 tbsp light soy sauce
1 clove garlic, finely chopped
5ml/1 tsp light brown sugar
2–3 spring onions, finely chopped
2.5ml/½ tsp finely chopped fresh
  root ginger
ground Szechuan pepper

1 Cut the beef into matchstick-sized strips. Thinly shred the carrots and celery sticks.

2 Heat the sesame oil in a preheated wok (it will smoke very quickly). Reduce the heat and stir-fry the beef shreds with the rice wine or sherry until the colour changes.

3 Pour off the excess liquid and reserve. Continue stirring until the meat is absolutely dry.

4 Add the chilli bean sauce, soy sauce, garlic and sugar. Blend well, then add the carrot and celery shreds. Increase the heat to high and add the spring onions, ginger and the reserved liquid. Continue stirring, and when all the juice has evaporated, season with Szechuan pepper and serve.

Mixed Vegetable Pickle

If you can obtain fresh turmeric, it makes such a difference to the colour and appearance of *Acar Campur*. You can use almost any vegetable, bearing in mind that you need a balance of textures, flavours and colours.

INGREDIENTS

Makes 2–3 x 300g/11oz jars

1 fresh red chilli, seeded and sliced
1 onion, quartered
2 garlic cloves, crushed
1cm/½ in cube *terasi*
4 macadamia nuts or 8 almonds
2.5cm/1in fresh turmeric, peeled and
    sliced, or 5ml/1 tsp ground turmeric
50ml/2fl oz/¼ cup sunflower oil
475ml/16fl oz/2 cups white vinegar
250ml/8fl oz/1 cup water
25–50g/1–2oz granulated sugar
3 carrots
225g/8oz green beans
1 small cauliflower
1 cucumber
225g/8oz white cabbage
115g/4oz dry-roasted peanuts,
    roughly crushed
salt

1 Place the chilli, onion, garlic, *terasi*, nuts and turmeric in a food processor and blend to a paste, or pound in a mortar with a pestle.

2 Heat the oil and stir-fry the paste to release the aroma. Add the vinegar, water, sugar and salt. Bring to the boil. Simmer for 10 minutes.

3 Cut the carrots into flower shapes. Cut the green beans into short, neat lengths. Separate the cauliflower into neat, bitesize florets. Peel and seed the cucumber and cut the flesh in neat, bitesize pieces. Cut the cabbage in neat, bitesize pieces.

4 Blanch each vegetable separately, in a large pan of boiling water, for 1 minute. Transfer to a colander and rinse with cold water, to halt the cooking. Drain well.

--- COOK'S TIP ---

This pickle is even better if you make it a few days ahead.

5 Add the vegetables to the sauce. Slowly bring to the boil and allow to cook for 5–10 minutes. Do not overcook – the vegetables should still be crunchy.

6 Add the peanuts and cool. Spoon into clean jars with lids.

Spiced Lamb with Spinach

INGREDIENTS

Serves 3–4

45ml/3 tbsp vegetable oil
500g/1¼lb lean boneless lamb, cut into
  2.5cm/1in cubes
1 onion, chopped
3 garlic cloves, finely chopped
1cm/½in fresh root ginger,
  finely chopped
6 black peppercorns
4 whole cloves
1 bay leaf
3 green cardamom pods, crushed
5ml/1 tsp ground cumin
5ml/1 tsp ground coriander
generous pinch of cayenne pepper
150ml/¼ pint/⅔ cup water
2 tomatoes, peeled, seeded
  and chopped
5ml/1 tsp salt
400g/14oz fresh spinach, trimmed,
  washed and finely chopped
5ml/1 tsp garam masala
crisp-fried onions and fresh coriander
  sprigs, to garnish
naan bread or spiced basmati rice,
  to serve

1 Heat a wok until hot. Add 30ml/
2 tbsp of the oil and swirl it
around. When hot, stir-fry the lamb in
batches until evenly browned. Remove
the lamb and set aside. Add the
remaining oil, onion, garlic and ginger
and stir-fry for 2–3 minutes.

2 Add the peppercorns, cloves,
bay leaf, cardamom pods, cumin,
ground coriander and cayenne pepper.
Stir-fry for 30–45 seconds. Return the
lamb and add the water, tomatoes and
salt and bring to the boil. Simmer,
covered, over a very low heat for about
1 hour, stirring occasionally until the
meat is cooked and tender.

3 Increase the heat, then gradually
add the spinach to the lamb,
stirring to mix. Keep stirring and
cooking until the spinach wilts
completely and most, but not all, of the
liquid has evaporated and you are left
with a thick green sauce. Stir in the
garam masala. Garnish with crisp-fried
onions and coriander sprigs. Serve with
naan bread or spiced basmati rice.

Spiced Coconut Mushrooms

Here is a simple and delicious way to cook mushrooms. They can be served with almost any oriental meal as well as with traditional western grilled or roasted meats and poultry.

INGREDIENTS

Serves 4

30ml/2 tbsp groundnut oil
2 garlic cloves, finely chopped
2 fresh red chillies, seeded and sliced
   into rings
3 shallots, finely chopped
225g/8oz brown-cap mushrooms,
   thickly sliced
150ml/¼ pint/⅔ cup coconut milk
30ml/2 tbsp chopped fresh coriander
salt and ground black pepper

1 Heat a wok until hot, add the oil and swirl it round the wok. Add the garlic and chillies, then stir-fry for a few seconds.

2 Add the shallots and stir-fry for 2–3 minutes until softened. Add the mushrooms and stir-fry for 3 minutes.

————— COOK'S TIP —————

Use snipped fresh chives instead of chopped fresh coriander, if you wish.

3 Pour in the coconut milk and bring to the boil. Boil rapidly over a high heat until the liquid has reduced by about half and coats the mushrooms. Season to taste with salt and pepper.

4 Sprinkle over the chopped coriander and toss the mushrooms gently to mix. Serve at once.

Glazed Lamb

Lemon and honey make a classical stir-fry combination in sweet dishes, and this lamb recipe shows how well they work together in savoury dishes, too. Serve with a fresh mixed salad to complete this delicious dish.

INGREDIENTS

Serves 4

450g/1lb boneless lean lamb
15ml/1 tbsp grapeseed oil
175g/6oz mangetouts, topped
  and tailed
3 spring onions, sliced
30ml/2 tbsp clear honey
juice of ½ lemon
30ml/2 tbsp chopped fresh coriander
15ml/1 tbsp sesame seeds
salt and ground black pepper

1 Using a cleaver, cut the lamb into thin strips.

COOK'S TIP

This recipe would work just as well made with pork or chicken instead of lamb. You could substitute chopped fresh basil for the coriander if using chicken.

2 Heat the wok, then add the oil. When the oil is hot, stir-fry the lamb until browned all over. Remove from the wok and keep warm.

3 Add the mangetouts and spring onions to the hot wok and stir-fry for 30 seconds.

4 Return the lamb to the wok and add the honey, lemon juice, chopped coriander and sesame seeds and season well. Stir thoroughly to mix. Bring to the boil, then allow to bubble vigorously for 1 minute until the lamb is completely coated in the honey mixture. Serve immediately.

Root Vegetables with Spiced Salt

All kinds of root vegetables can be finely sliced and deep-fried to make "crisps". Serve as an accompaniment to an oriental-style meal or simply by themselves as much tastier nibbles than commercial snacks with pre-dinner drinks.

INGREDIENTS

Serves 4–6
1 carrot
2 parsnips
2 raw beetroots
1 sweet potato
groundnut oil, for deep-frying
1.5ml/¼ tsp chilli powder
5ml/1 tsp sea salt flakes

1 Peel the carrot, parsnips, beetroots and sweet potato. Slice the carrot and parsnips into long, thin ribbons. Cut the beetroots and sweet potato into thin rounds. Pat dry on kitchen paper.

2 Half-fill a wok with oil and heat to 180°C/350°F. Add the vegetable slices in batches and deep-fry for 2–3 minutes until golden and crisp. Remove and drain on kitchen paper.

3 Place the chilli powder and sea salt flakes in a mortar and grind them together with a pestle to form a coarse powder.

4 Pile up the vegetable "crisps" on a serving plate and sprinkle over the spiced salt.

--- COOK'S TIP ---

To save time, you can slice the vegetables using a mandoline, blender or food processor with a thin slicing disc attached.

Balti Lamb Tikka

One of the best ways of tenderizing meat is to marinate it in papaya, which must be unripe or it will lend too much sweetness to what should be a savoury dish. Papaya, also known as pawpaw, is readily available from most large supermarkets.

INGREDIENTS

Serves 4

675g/1½lb lean lamb, cubed
1 unripe papaya
45ml/3 tbsp natural yogurt
5ml/1 tsp ginger pulp
5ml/1 tsp chilli powder
5ml/1 tsp garlic pulp
1.5ml/¼ tsp ground turmeric
10ml/2 tsp ground coriander
5ml/1 tsp ground cumin
30ml/2 tbsp lemon juice
15ml/1 tbsp chopped fresh coriander,
   plus extra for garnishing
1.5ml/¼ tsp red food colouring
300ml/½ pint/1¼ cups corn oil
salt
lemon wedges and onion rings,
   to garnish
raita and naan, to serve

1 Place the cubed lamb in a large mixing bowl. Peel the papaya, cut in half and scoop out the seeds. Cut the flesh into cubes, place in a food processor or blender and blend until it is pulped, adding about 15ml/1 tbsp water if necessary.

2 Pour about 30ml/2 tbsp of the papaya pulp over the lamb cubes and rub it in well with your fingers. Set aside to marinate for at least 3 hours.

3 Meanwhile, mix together the yogurt, ginger, chilli powder, garlic, turmeric, ground coriander, cumin, lemon juice, fresh coriander, red food colouring and 30ml/2 tbsp of the oil. Season with salt and set aside.

4 Spoon the yogurt mixture over the lamb and mix together well.

5 Heat the remaining oil in a wok. When it is hot, lower the heat slightly and add the lamb cubes, a few at a time. Deep-fry the batches of lamb for 5–7 minutes or until the lamb is cooked and tender. Transfer each batch to a warmed serving dish and keep warm while you cook the next batch.

6 When all the batches of lamb have been cooked, garnish with the lemon wedges, onion rings and fresh coriander. Serve with raita and naan.

Szechuan Aubergines

INGREDIENTS

Serves 4

2 small aubergines
5ml/1 tsp salt
3 dried red chillies
groundnut oil, for deep-frying
3–4 garlic cloves, finely chopped
1cm/½in fresh root ginger,
　finely chopped
4 spring onions, chopped and white
　and green parts separated
15ml/1 tbsp Chinese rice wine or
　dry sherry
15ml/1 tbsp light soy sauce
5ml/1 tsp sugar
1.5ml/¼ tsp ground roasted
　Szechuan peppercorns
15ml/1 tbsp Chinese rice vinegar
5ml/1 tsp sesame oil

1 Trim the aubergines and cut into strips, about 4cm/1½in wide and 7.5cm/3in long. Place the aubergines in a colander and sprinkle with the salt. Leave for 30 minutes, then rinse them thoroughly under cold running water. Pat dry with kitchen paper.

2 Meanwhile soak the chillies in warm water for 15 minutes. Drain, then cut each chilli into three or four pieces, discarding the seeds.

3 Half-fill a wok with oil and heat to 180°C/350°F. Deep-fry the aubergine until golden brown. Drain on kitchen paper. Pour off most of the oil from the wok. Reheat the oil and add the garlic, ginger and white part of the spring onions.

4 Stir-fry for 30 seconds. Add the aubergine and toss, then add the wine or sherry, soy sauce, sugar, ground Szechuan peppercorns and rice vinegar. Stir-fry for 1–2 minutes. Sprinkle over the sesame oil and green spring onion.

Stuffed Green Peppers

Stuffed peppers are given a different treatment here where they are deep-fried in a wok and served with a tangy sauce.

INGREDIENTS

Serves 4

225–275g/8–10oz minced pork
4–6 water chestnuts, finely chopped
2 spring onions, finely chopped
2.5ml/½ tsp finely chopped fresh
   root ginger
15ml/1 tbsp light soy sauce
15ml/1 tbsp Chinese rice wine or
   dry sherry
3–4 green peppers, cored and seeded
15ml/1 tbsp cornflour
vegetable oil, for deep-frying

For the sauce

10ml/2 tsp light soy sauce
5ml/1 tsp light brown sugar
1–2 fresh hot chillies, finely
   chopped (optional)
about 75ml/5 tbsp stock or water

1 Mix together the minced pork, water chestnuts, spring onions, ginger, soy sauce and rice wine or sherry in a bowl.

— COOK'S TIP —

You could substitute minced beef or lamb for the minced pork used in this recipe.

2 Cut the green peppers into halves or quarters. Stuff the sections with the pork mixture and sprinkle with a little cornflour.

3 Heat the oil in a preheated wok and deep-fry the stuffed peppers, with the meat side down, for 2–3 minutes, then remove and drain.

4 Pour off the excess oil, then return the stuffed green peppers to the wok with the meat side up. Add the sauce ingredients, shaking the wok gently to make sure they do not stick to the bottom, and braise for 2–3 minutes. Carefully lift the stuffed peppers on to a serving dish, meat side up, and pour the sauce over them.

Stir-fried Greens

Quail's eggs look very attractive in *Chah Kang Kung*, but you can substitute some baby sweetcorn, halved at an angle.

INGREDIENTS

Serves 4

2 bunches spinach or chard or 1 head
    Chinese leaves or 450g/1lb curly kale
3 garlic cloves, crushed
5cm/2in fresh root ginger, peeled and
    cut in matchsticks
45–60ml/3–4 tbsp groundnut oil
115g/4oz boneless, skinless chicken
    breast, or pork fillet, or a mixture of
    both, very finely sliced
12 quail's eggs, hard-boiled and shelled
1 fresh red chilli, seeded and shredded
30–45ml/2–3 tbsp oyster sauce
15ml/1 tbsp brown sugar
10ml/2 tsp cornflour, mixed with
    50ml/2fl oz/¼ cup cold water
salt

COOK'S TIP

As with all stir-fries, don't start cooking until you have prepared all the ingredients and arranged them to hand. Cut everything into small, even-size pieces so the food can be cooked very quickly and all the colours and flavours preserved.

1 Wash the chosen leaves well and shake them dry. Strip the tender leaves from the stems and tear them into pieces. Discard the lower, tougher part of the stems and slice the remainder evenly.

2 Fry the garlic and ginger in the hot oil, without browning, for a minute. Add the chicken and/or pork and keep stirring it in the wok until the meat changes colour. When the meat looks cooked, add the sliced stems first and cook them quickly; then add the torn leaves, quail's eggs and chilli. Spoon in the oyster sauce and a little boiling water, if necessary. Cover and cook for 1–2 minutes only.

3 Remove the cover, stir and add sugar and salt to taste. Stir in the cornflour and water mixture and toss thoroughly. Cook until the mixture is well coated in a glossy sauce.

4 Serve immediately, while still very hot and the colours are bright and positively jewel-like.

Stir-fried Pork with Vegetables

This is a basic recipe for stir-frying any meat with any vegetables, according to seasonal availability and preference.

INGREDIENTS

Serves 4
225g/8oz pork fillet
15ml/1 tbsp light soy sauce
5ml/1 tsp light brown sugar
5ml/1 tsp Chinese rice wine or
  dry sherry
10ml/2 tsp cornflour paste
115g/4oz mangetouts
115g/4oz white mushrooms
1 carrot
1 spring onion
60ml/4 tbsp vegetable oil
5ml/1 tsp salt
stock (optional)
few drops sesame oil

1 Cut the pork into thin slices, each about the size of a postage stamp. Marinate with about 5ml/1 tsp of the soy sauce, sugar, rice wine or sherry and cornflour paste.

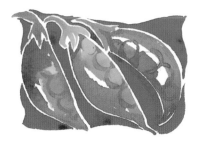

2 Top and tail the mangetouts. Thinly slice the mushrooms. Cut the carrot into pieces roughly the same size as the pork and cut the spring onion into short sections.

3 Heat the oil in a preheated wok and stir-fry the pork for about 1 minute or until its colour changes. Remove with a slotted spoon and keep warm while you cook the vegetables.

4 Add the vegetables to the wok and stir-fry for about 2 minutes. Add the salt and the partly cooked pork, and a little stock or water if necessary. Continue cooking and stirring for about 1 minute, then add the remaining soy sauce and blend well. Sprinkle with the sesame oil and serve.

Crispy Cabbage

This makes a wonderful accompaniment to meat or vegetable dishes – just a couple of spoonfuls adds a crunchy texture to a meal. It goes especially well with prawn dishes.

INGREDIENTS

Serves 4
4 juniper berries
1 large Savoy cabbage
60ml/4 tbsp vegetable oil
1 clove garlic, crushed
5ml/1 tsp caster sugar
5ml/1 tsp salt

1 Finely crush the juniper berries, in a mortar with a pestle.

2 Finely shred the cabbage.

3 Heat a wok, then add the oil. When the oil is hot, stir-fry the garlic for 1 minute. Add the cabbage and stir-fry for 3–4 minutes until crispy. Remove from the wok and pat dry with kitchen paper.

4 Reheat the wok and return the cabbage to it. Add the sugar, salt and crushed juniper berries and toss the cabbage so that it is well coated and thoroughly mixed with the flavourings. Serve either hot or cold.

POULTRY

Poultry, especially chicken, is probably the most versatile of ingredients, and this collection of palate-tingling dishes fully explores its vast range. Recipes include classics, such as Szechuan chicken and a delicious Indonesian satay; family favourites, such as sweet and sour chicken and chicken and cashew nuts; and some more unfamiliar and adventurous dishes, such as sweet-sour duck with mango and Balti baby chicken in tamarind sauce. From the delicately flavoured and aromatic to the fiery hot and spicy, there is something here to please everyone.

Karahi Shredded Cabbage with Cumin

This cabbage is only lightly spiced and makes a good accompaniment to most other Balti dishes.

INGREDIENTS

Serves 4

15ml/1 tbsp corn oil
50g/2oz butter
2.5ml/½ tsp crushed coriander seeds
2.5ml/½ tsp white cumin seeds
6 dried red chillies
1 small Savoy cabbage, shredded
12 mangetouts
3 fresh red chillies, seeded and sliced
12 baby sweetcorn
salt
25g/1oz flaked almonds, toasted
   and 15ml/1 tbsp chopped fresh
   coriander, to garnish

1 Heat the oil and butter in a preheated wok and, when the butter has melted, add the crushed coriander seeds, cumin seeds and dried red chillies.

2 Add the shredded cabbage and mangetouts to the wok and stir-fry for about 5 minutes.

3 Add the fresh red chillies, baby sweetcorn and salt and stir-fry for a further 3 minutes.

4 Garnish the cabbage with toasted almonds and fresh coriander and serve hot.

COOK'S TIP

Unlike many parts of the Indian sub-continent, Pakistan – whence Balti recipes come – is generally a meat-eating nation. Vegetable dishes are, therefore, usually cooked as side dishes, rather than as a main dish, much in the way they are in the West. Consequently, this delicious, slightly spicy treatment of cabbage would go as well with a traditional western roast as it would with a Balti curry or stir-fry.

Fu-yung Chicken

Because the egg whites mixed with milk are deep-fried in a wok, they have prompted some imaginative cooks to refer to this dish as "Deep-fried Milk"!

INGREDIENTS

Serves 4

175g/6oz chicken breast fillet, skinned
5ml/1 tsp salt
4 egg whites, lightly beaten
15ml/1 tbsp cornflour paste
30ml/2 tbsp milk
vegetable oil, for deep-frying
1 lettuce heart, separated into leaves
about 120ml/4fl oz/½ cup stock
15ml/1 tbsp Chinese rice wine or
    dry sherry
15ml/1 tbsp green peas
few drops sesame oil
5ml/1 tsp minced ham, to garnish

1 Finely mince the chicken meat, then mix with a pinch of the salt, the egg whites, cornflour paste and milk. Blend well until smooth.

2 Heat the oil in a very hot wok, but before the oil gets too hot, gently spoon the chicken and egg white mixture into the oil in batches. Do not stir, otherwise it will scatter. Stir the oil from the bottom of the wok so that the egg whites will rise to the surface. Remove as soon as the colour turns bright white. Drain.

3 Pour off the excess oil, leaving about 15ml/1 tbsp in the wok. Stir-fry the lettuce leaves with the remaining salt for 1 minute, add the stock and bring to the boil.

4 Add the chicken to the wok with the rice wine and peas, and blend well. Sprinkle with sesame oil, garnish with ham and serve immediately.

Szechuan Spicy Tofu

The meat used in this popular wok recipe can be omitted to create a purely vegetarian dish, if you prefer.

Ingredients

Serves 4

3 packets tofu
1 leek
45ml/3 tbsp vegetable oil
115g/4oz minced beef
15ml/1 tbsp black bean sauce
15ml/1 tbsp light soy sauce
5ml/1 tsp chilli bean sauce
15ml/1 tbsp Chinese rice wine or
  dry sherry
about 45–60ml/3–4 tbsp stock or water
10ml/2 tsp cornflour paste
ground Szechuan peppercorns, to taste
few drops of sesame oil

1 Cut the tofu into 1cm/½in square cubes. Fill a wok with boiling water, add the tofu cubes and bring back to the boil. Cook for 2–3 minutes to harden. Remove and drain. Cut the leek into short sections.

2 Empty the wok. Preheat and add the oil. When hot, stir-fry the minced beef until the colour changes, then add the leek and black bean sauce. Add the tofu with the soy sauce, chilli bean sauce and rice wine or sherry. Stir gently for 1 minute.

3 Add the stock or water, bring to the boil and braise for 2-3 minutes.

4 Stir in the cornflour paste and cook, stirring, until thickened. Season with ground Szechuan pepper, sprinkle with the sesame oil and serve immediately.

Szechuan Chicken

A wok is the ideal cooking pot for this stir-fried chicken dish. The flavours emerge wonderfully and the chicken is fresh and crisp.

INGREDIENTS

Serves 4

350g/12oz chicken thigh, boned
    and skinned
1.5ml/¼ tsp salt
½ egg white, lightly beaten
10ml/2 tsp cornflour paste
1 green pepper, cored and seeded
60ml/4 tbsp vegetable oil
3–4 whole dried red chillies, soaked in
    water for 10 minutes
1 spring onion, cut into short sections
few small pieces of fresh root
    ginger, peeled
15ml/1 tbsp sweet bean paste or
    hoi-sin sauce
5ml/1 tsp chilli bean paste
15ml/1 tbsp Chinese rice wine or
    dry sherry
115g/4oz roasted cashew nuts
few drops sesame oil

1 Cut the chicken meat into small cubes, each about the size of a sugar lump. Mix together the chicken, salt, egg white and cornflour paste in a bowl.

2 Cut the green pepper into cubes about the same size as the chicken.

3 Heat the oil in a preheated wok. Stir-fry the chicken cubes for about 1 minute, or until the colour changes. Remove from the wok with a slotted spoon and keep warm.

4 Add the green pepper, chillies, spring onion and ginger and stir-fry for about 1 minute. Then add the chicken, sweet bean paste or hoi-sin sauce, chilli bean paste and rice wine or sherry. Blend well and cook for 1 minute more. Finally add the cashew nuts and sesame oil. Serve hot.

Aubergine in Spicy Sauce

Aubergines are given a royal treatment in this recipe, where they are stir-fried with seasonings more commonly associated with fish cooking.

INGREDIENTS

Serves 4

450g/1lb aubergines
3–4 whole dried red chillies, soaked in water for 10 minutes
vegetable oil, for deep-frying
1 clove garlic, finely chopped
5ml/1 tsp finely chopped fresh ginger
5ml/1 tsp finely chopped spring onion, white part only
115g/4oz lean pork, shredded (optional)
15ml/1 tbsp light soy sauce
15ml/1 tbsp light brown sugar
15ml/1 tbsp chilli bean sauce
15ml/1 tbsp Chinese rice wine or dry sherry
15ml/1 tbsp rice vinegar
10ml/2 tsp cornflour paste, see Cook's Tip, Chinese Crispy Spring Rolls
5ml/1 tsp finely chopped spring onions, green part only, to garnish
few drops sesame oil

1 Cut the aubergines into short strips the size of chips – the skin can either be peeled off or left on, whichever you prefer. Cut the soaked red chillies into two or three small pieces and discard the seeds.

2 Heat the oil in a preheated wok and deep-fry the aubergine chips for about 3–4 minutes or until limp. Remove and drain.

3 Pour off the excess oil, leaving about 15ml/1 tbsp in the wok. Add the garlic, ginger, white spring onions and chillies, stir a few times, then add the pork, if using. Stir-fry the meat for about 1 minute or until it becomes pale, almost white, in colour. Add all the seasonings, then increase the heat and bring the mixture to the boil.

4 Add the aubergines to the wok, blend well and braise for 30–40 seconds, then thicken the sauce with the cornflour paste, stirring until smooth. Garnish with the green spring onions and sprinkle with sesame oil.

COOK'S TIP

Soaking dried chillies in water will reduce their spicy flavour. If you prefer a milder chilli taste, soak for longer than the recommended 10 minutes.

Indonesian-style Satay Chicken

Satay traditionally forms part of a *Rijsttafel* – literally rice table – a vast feast of as many as 40 different dishes served with a large bowl of plain rice. However, for the less ambitious, creamy coconut satay makes these chicken pieces a mouth-watering dish to present at the table at any time of the day.

INGREDIENTS

Serves 4

50g/2oz raw peanuts
45ml/3 tbsp vegetable oil
1 small onion, finely chopped
2.5cm/1in fresh root ginger, peeled and
  finely chopped
1 clove garlic, crushed
675g/1½lb chicken thighs, skinned and
  cut into cubes
90g/3½oz creamed coconut,
  roughly chopped
15ml/1 tbsp chilli sauce
60ml/4 tbsp crunchy peanut butter
5ml/1 tsp soft dark brown sugar
150ml/¼ pint/⅔ cup milk
1.5ml/¼ tsp salt

2 Heat the wok and add 5ml/1 tsp oil. When the oil is hot, stir-fry the peanuts for 1 minute until crisp and golden. Remove with a slotted spoon and drain on kitchen paper.

3 Add the remaining oil to the hot wok. When the oil is hot, add the onion, ginger and garlic and stir-fry for 2–3 minutes until softened but not browned. Remove with a slotted spoon and drain on kitchen paper.

4 Add the chicken pieces to the wok and stir-fry for 3–4 minutes until crisp and golden on all sides. Thread on to pre-soaked bamboo skewers and keep warm.

5 Add the creamed coconut to the hot wok in small pieces and stir-fry until melted. Add the chilli sauce, peanut butter and ginger mixture and simmer for 2 minutes. Stir in the sugar, milk and salt, and simmer for a further 3 minutes. Serve the skewered chicken hot, with a dish of the hot dipping sauce sprinkled with the peanuts.

1 Shell the peanuts and remove the skins by rubbing them between the palms of the hands. Put them in a small bowl, add just enough water to cover and soak for 1 minute. Drain the nuts and cut them into slivers.

Braised Chinese Vegetables

The original recipe calls for no less than 18 different ingredients to represent the 18 Buddhas (*Lo Han*). Later, this was reduced to eight, but nowadays anything between four and six items is regarded as quite sufficient to put in a wok.

INGREDIENTS

Serves 4

10g/¼oz dried Chinese mushrooms
75g/3oz straw mushrooms
75g/3oz sliced bamboo shoots, drained
50g/2oz mangetouts
1 packet tofu
175g/6oz Chinese leaves
45–60ml/3–4 tbsp vegetable oil
5ml/1 tsp salt
2.5ml/½ tsp light brown sugar
15ml/1 tbsp light soy sauce
few drops sesame oil

1 Soak the Chinese mushrooms in cold water for 20–25 minutes, then rinse and discard the hard stalks, if any. Cut the straw mushrooms in half lengthways, if they are large, keep them whole, if they are small. Rinse and drain the bamboo shoot slices. Top and tail the mangetouts. Cut the tofu into about 12 small pieces. Cut the Chinese leaves into small pieces about the same size as the mangetouts.

2 Harden the tofu pieces by placing them in a wok of boiling water for about 2 minutes. Remove and drain.

3 Discard the water and heat the oil in the wok, a saucepan or a flameproof casserole. Lightly brown the tofu pieces on both sides. Remove with a slotted spoon and keep warm.

4 Stir-fry all the vegetables in the wok or pan for about 1½ minutes, then add the tofu, salt, sugar and soy sauce. Continue stirring for 1 minute, then cover and braise for 2–3 minutes. Sprinkle with sesame oil and serve.

Hot Chilli Chicken

A tantalizing mixture of lemon grass and ginger provides the flavourings for this chicken feast. The ingredients are gently simmered in a wok to achieve a superb end effect.

INGREDIENTS

Serves 4–6

3 chicken legs, thighs and drumsticks
15ml/1 tbsp vegetable oil
2cm/³/₄in fresh root ginger, peeled and finely chopped
1 clove garlic, crushed
1 small red chilli, seeded and finely chopped
5cm/2in lemon grass stalk, shredded
150ml/¹/₄ pint/²/₃ cup chicken stock
15ml/1 tbsp fish sauce (optional)
10ml/2 tsp sugar
2.5ml/¹/₂ tsp salt
juice of ¹/₂ lemon
50g/2oz raw peanuts
2 spring onions, shredded
rind of 1 mandarin orange or satsuma, shredded
30ml/2 tbsp chopped fresh mint, to garnish
rice or rice noodles, to serve

1 With the heel of the knife, chop through the narrow end of the drumsticks. Remove the jointed parts of the drumsticks and thigh bones, then remove the skin.

2 Heat the oil in a large preheated wok. Add the chicken, ginger, garlic, chilli and lemon grass and cook for 3–4 minutes. Add the chicken stock, fish sauce, if using, sugar, salt and lemon juice. Lower the heat, cover and simmer for 30–35 minutes.

3 To prepare the peanuts for the topping, grill or roast them under a steady heat until evenly brown, for about 2–3 minutes. Turn the nuts out on to a dish towel and rub briskly to loosen the skins.

4 Serve the chicken scattered with roasted peanuts, shredded spring onions and the rind of the mandarin orange or satsuma. Garnish with mint and serve with rice or rice noodles.

--- COOK'S TIP ---

This dish can also be prepared using duck legs. Be sure to remove the jointed parts of the drumsticks and thigh bones to make the meat easier to eat with chopsticks.

Stir-fried Beansprouts

This is an easy way to cook up some tasty beansprouts in a wok. It is not necessary to top and tail them. Simply rinse in a bowl of cold water and discard any husks that float to the surface.

INGREDIENTS

Serves 4
2–3 spring onions
225g/8oz fresh beansprouts
45ml/3 tbsp vegetable oil
5ml/1 tsp salt
2.5ml/½ tsp light brown sugar
few drops sesame oil (optional)

1 Cut the spring onions into short sections about the same length as the beansprouts.

2 Heat the oil in a wok and stir-fry the beansprouts and spring onions for about 1 minute. Add the salt and sugar and continue stirring for 1 minute. Sprinkle with the sesame oil, if using, and serve. Do not overcook or the beansprouts will go soggy.

--- COOK'S TIP ---

Fresh and canned beansprouts are readily available, but they can easily be grown at home for a constant and completely fresh supply. Scatter mung beans on several layers of damp kitchen paper on a small plate. Keep moist in a fairly warm place and the beans will sprout in a few days.

Stir-fried Chicken with Basil and Chillies

This quick and easy chicken dish is an excellent introduction to Thai cuisine. Deep-frying the basil adds another dimension to this dish. Thai basil, which is sometimes known as Holy basil, has a unique, pungent flavour that is both spicy and sharp. The dull leaves have serrated edges.

INGREDIENTS

Serves 4–6

45ml/3 tbsp vegetable oil
4 garlic cloves, sliced
2–4 red chillies, seeded and chopped
450g/1lb chicken, cut into
  bite-size pieces
30–45ml/2–3 tbsp fish sauce
10ml/2 tsp dark soy sauce
5ml/1 tsp sugar
10–12 Thai basil leaves
2 red chillies, finely sliced, to garnish
20 Thai basil leaves, deep-fried
  (optional)

1 Heat the oil in a wok or large frying pan and swirl it around.

2 Add the garlic and chillies and stir-fry until golden.

3 Add the chicken and stir-fry until it changes colour.

4 Season with fish sauce, soy sauce and sugar. Continue to stir-fry for 3-4 minutes or until the chicken is cooked. Stir in the fresh Thai basil leaves. Garnish with sliced chillies and the deep-fried basil, if using.

COOK'S TIP

To deep-fry Thai basil leaves, make sure that the leaves are completely dry. Deep-fry in hot oil for about 30–40 seconds, lift out and drain on kitchen paper.

Stir-fried Chinese Leaves with Mushrooms

You can stir-fry fresh button mushrooms in this recipe if you prefer them, or if fresh or canned straw mushrooms are not available.

INGREDIENTS

Serves 4

225g/8oz fresh straw mushrooms or
    350g/12oz canned straw
    mushrooms, drained
60ml/4 tbsp vegetable oil
400g/14oz Chinese leaves, cut
    in strips
5ml/1 tsp salt
5ml/1 tsp light brown sugar
15ml/1tbsp cornflour paste
120ml/4fl oz/½ cup milk

1 Cut the mushrooms in half lengthways. Heat half the oil, stir-fry the Chinese leaves for 2 minutes, then add half the salt and half the sugar. Stir for 1 minute.

2 Transfer the Chinese leaves to a warm serving dish. Add the mushrooms to the wok and stir-fry for 1 minute. Add the remaining salt and sugar, cook for 1 minute, then thicken with the cornflour paste and milk. Serve with the Chinese leaves.

--- COOK'S TIP ---

The Chinese approach cooking with the same overall desire for harmony and balance that characterizes their ancient philosophy. Recipes for stir-fried vegetables are not simply an arbitrary combination of whatever is to hand – they should balance and complement each other in both colour and texture. The delicious slipperiness of straw mushrooms complements the crunchier texture of the Chinese leaves, so it is best to use them if at all possible. Canned straw mushrooms are available from oriental food stores. Do not overcook or the harmony and balance will be lost.

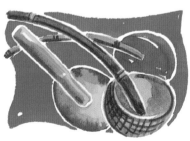

Chicken and Cashew Nut Stir-fry

Hoi-sin sauce lends a sweet yet slightly hot note to this chicken stir-fry, while cashew nuts add a pleasing contrast of texture.

INGREDIENTS

Serves 4

75g/3oz cashew nuts
1 red pepper
450g/1lb skinless chicken breast fillets
45ml/3 tbsp groundnut oil
4 garlic cloves, finely chopped
30ml/2 tbsp Chinese rice wine or
   dry sherry
45ml/3 tbsp hoi-sin sauce
10ml/2 tsp sesame oil
5–6 spring onions, green parts only,
   cut into 2.5cm/1in lengths

1 Heat a wok until hot, add the cashew nuts and dry-fry over a low to medium heat for 1–2 minutes until golden brown. Remove and set aside.

2 Cut the red pepper in half and remove the core and seeds. Slice into thin strips. Cut the chicken fillet into thin finger-length strips.

3 Heat the wok again until hot, add the oil and swirl it around. Add the garlic and let it sizzle in the oil for a few seconds. Add the pepper and chicken and stir-fry for 2 minutes.

4 Add the rice wine or sherry and hoi-sin sauce. Continue to stir-fry until the chicken is tender and all the ingredients are evenly glazed.

5 Stir in the sesame oil, toasted cashew nuts and spring onion tips. Serve immediately.

> ——— COOK'S TIP ———
>
> Use blanched almonds instead of cashew nuts, if you prefer. If you prefer a slightly less sweet taste, you could substitute light soy sauce for the hoi-sin sauce.

VEGETABLE DISHES

Vegetables particularly benefit from fast cooking in a wok, as this helps to preserve their texture and colour, as well as their nutritional content. This exciting collection of recipes includes some standard and familiar accompaniments to main-course dishes, such as potatoes, broccoli and onions, and simultaneously suggests some unusual vegetable dishes with more exotic ingredients and sauces. All of them are cooked in intriguing ways that lend themselves to oriental meals, as well as more traditional western roasts, grills and fish dishes.

Chicken, Ham and Broccoli Stir-fry

The charmingly poetic Chinese name for this pretty and colourful dish – *Jin Hua Yi Shu Ji* – means "golden flower and jade tree chicken". It is a marvellous, cold-buffet-style stir-fry to serve on any occasion.

INGREDIENTS

Serves 6–8

1 chicken, about 1–1.35kg/2¼–3lb
2 spring onions
2–3 pieces fresh root ginger
15ml/1 tbsp salt
225g/8oz honey-roast ham
285g/10oz broccoli
45ml/3 tbsp vegetable oil
5ml/1 tsp light brown sugar
10ml/2 tsp cornflour

1 Place the chicken in a large pan and cover it with cold water. Add the spring onions, ginger and about 10ml/2 tsp of the salt. Bring to the boil, then reduce the heat and simmer for 10–15 minutes under a tightly fitting lid. Turn off the heat and let the chicken cook itself in the hot water for at least 4–5 hours; do not lift the lid as this will let out the residual heat.

2 Remove the chicken from the pan, reserving the liquid, and carefully cut the meat away from the bones, keeping the skin on. Slice both the chicken and ham into pieces, each the size of a matchbox, and arrange the meats in alternating layers on a plate.

3 Cut the broccoli into small florets and stir-fry in the hot oil with the remaining salt and the sugar for about 2–3 minutes. Arrange the broccoli between the rows of chicken and ham and around the edge of the plate, making a border for the meat.

4 Heat 30ml/2tbsp of the chicken stock and thicken it with the cornflour. Stir until smooth, then pour it evenly all over the chicken and ham to form a thin coat of transparent jelly. Allow to cool before serving.

Stir-fried Turkey with Broccoli and Mushrooms

This is a really easy, tasty supper dish which works well with chicken too.

INGREDIENTS

Serves 4

115g/4oz broccoli florets
4 spring onions
5ml/1 tsp cornflour
45ml/3 tbsp oyster sauce
15ml/1 tbsp dark soy sauce
120ml/4fl oz/$\frac{1}{2}$ cup chicken stock
10ml/2 tsp lemon juice
45ml/3 tbsp groundnut oil
450g/1lb turkey steaks cut into strips, about 5mm x 5cm/$\frac{1}{4}$ x 2in
1 small onion, chopped
2 garlic cloves, crushed
10ml/2 tsp grated fresh root ginger
115g/4oz fresh shiitake mushrooms, sliced
75g/3oz baby sweetcorn, halved lengthways
15ml/1 tbsp sesame oil
salt and ground black pepper
egg noodles, to serve

2 Finely chop the white parts of the spring onions and slice the green parts into thin shreds.

3 In a bowl, blend together the cornflour, oyster sauce, soy sauce, stock and lemon juice. Set aside.

4 Heat 30ml/2 tbsp of the groundnut oil in a preheated wok. Add the turkey and stir-fry for 2 minutes until golden and crisp at the edges. Remove from the wok and keep warm.

5 Add the remaining groundnut oil to the wok and stir-fry the chopped onion, garlic and ginger over a medium heat for about 1 minute. Increase the heat to high, add the broccoli, mushrooms and sweetcorn and stir-fry for 2 minutes.

6 Return the turkey to the wok, then add the sauce with the chopped spring onion and seasoning. Cook, stirring, for about 1 minute until the sauce has thickened. Stir in the sesame oil. Serve immediately on a bed of egg noodles with the finely shredded spring onion scattered on top.

1 Divide the broccoli florets into smaller sprigs and cut the stalks into thin diagonal slices.

Stir-fried Sweet and Sour Chicken

This all-in-one stir-fry has a South-east Asian influence, and it is ideal for today's cook who is so often short of time.

INGREDIENTS

Serves 4

275g/10oz Chinese egg noodles
30ml/2 tbsp vegetable oil
3 spring onions, chopped
1 garlic clove, crushed
2.5cm/1in fresh root ginger, peeled and grated
5ml/1 tsp hot paprika
5ml/1 tsp ground coriander
3 chicken breast fillets, sliced
115g/4oz sugar snap peas, topped and tailed
115g/4oz baby sweetcorn, halved
225g/8oz fresh beansprouts
15ml/1 tbsp cornflour
45ml/3 tbsp soy sauce
45ml/3 tbsp lemon juice
15ml/1 tbsp sugar
salt
45ml/3 tbsp chopped fresh coriander or spring onion tops, to garnish

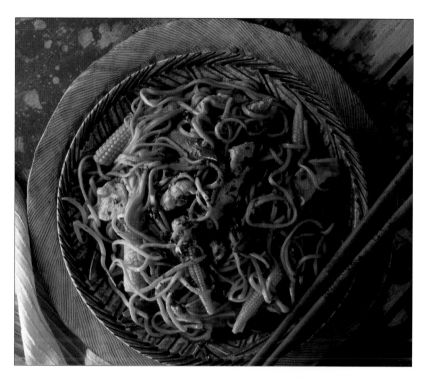

1 Bring a large saucepan of salted water to the boil. Add the noodles and cook according to the packet instructions if using dried noodles. If using fresh egg noodles, cook for a few minutes only, stirring occasionally to separate. Drain thoroughly, cover and keep warm.

2 Heat the oil in a pre-heated wok. Add the spring onions and cook over a gentle heat. Mix in the garlic, ginger, paprika, coriander and chicken, then stir-fry for 3–4 minutes.

3 Add the peas, baby sweetcorn and beansprouts, cover and cook briefly. Add the noodles.

4 Combine the cornflour, soy sauce, lemon juice and sugar in a small bowl. Add to the wok and simmer briefly to thicken. Serve immediately, garnished with chopped coriander or spring onion tops.

COOK'S TIP

Large wok lids are cumbersome and can be difficult to store in a small kitchen. Consider placing a circle of greaseproof paper against the food surface to keep the cooking juices in.

Sweet-sour Duck with Mango

Mango adds natural sweetness to this colourful stir-fry. Crispy deep-fried noodles make the perfect accompaniment.

INGREDIENTS

Serves 4

225–350g/8–12oz duck breasts
45ml/3 tbsp dark soy sauce
15ml/1tbsp Chinese rice wine or
 dry sherry
5ml/1 tsp sesame oil
5ml/1 tsp Chinese five-spice powder
15ml/1 tbsp soft brown sugar
10ml/2 tsp cornflour
45ml/3 tbsp Chinese rice vinegar
15ml/1 tbsp tomato ketchup
1 mango, not too ripe
3 baby aubergines
1 red onion
1 carrot
60ml/4 tbsp groundnut oil
1 garlic clove, sliced
2.5cm/1in fresh root ginger, cut
 into shreds
75g/3oz sugar snap peas

1 Thinly slice the duck breasts and place in a bowl. Mix together 15ml/1 tbsp of the soy sauce with the rice wine or sherry, sesame oil and five-spice powder. Pour over the duck, cover and leave to marinate for 1–2 hours. In a separate bowl, blend together the sugar, cornflour, rice vinegar, ketchup and remaining soy sauce. Set aside.

2 Peel the mango, slice the flesh from the stone, then cut into thick strips. Slice the aubergines, onion and carrot into similar-sized pieces.

3 Heat a wok until hot, add 30ml/ 2 tbsp of the oil and swirl it around. Drain the duck, reserving the marinade. Stir-fry the duck slices over a high heat until the fat is crisp and golden. Remove and keep warm. Add 15ml/1 tbsp of the oil to the wok and stir-fry the aubergine for 3 minutes until golden.

4 Add the remaining oil and fry the onion, garlic, ginger and carrot for 2–3 minutes, then add the sugar snap peas and stir fry for a further 2 minutes.

5 Add the mango and return the duck with the sauce and reserved marinade to the wok. Cook, stirring, until the sauce thickens slightly. Serve at once.

COOK'S TIP

If baby aubergines are not available, use the smallest you can find. Sprinkle with salt after slicing and set aside in a colander for the bitter juices to drain off. Rinse thoroughly before cooking.

Balti Chicken with Lentils

This is rather an unusual combination of flavours, but it is certainly worth trying! The mango powder gives a delicious tangy flavour to this spicy dish.

INGREDIENTS

Serves 4–6

75g/3oz split yellow lentils
60ml/4 tbsp corn oil
2 medium leeks, chopped
6 large dried red chillies
4 curry leaves
5ml/1 tsp mustard seeds
10ml/2 tsp mango powder
2 medium tomatoes, chopped
2.5ml/½ tsp chilli powder
5ml/1 tsp ground coriander
450g/1lb boneless chicken, skinned and cubed
salt
15ml/1 tbsp chopped fresh coriander, to garnish
paratha, to serve

1 Put the lentils in a sieve and wash carefully under plenty of cold running water.

2 Put the lentils in a saucepan and add just enough water to cover. Bring to the boil and cook for 10 minutes or until they are soft but not mushy. Drain thoroughly, transfer to a bowl and set aside.

3 Heat the oil in a preheated wok until hot. Lower the heat and add the leeks, dried red chillies, curry leaves and mustard seeds and stir-fry gently for 2–3 minutes.

4 Add the mango powder, tomatoes, chilli powder, ground coriander and chicken. Season with salt and stir-fry for 7–10 minutes.

5 Mix in the cooked lentils and fry for a further 2 minutes or until the chicken is cooked through.

6 Garnish with fresh coriander and serve immediately with paratha.

Duck with Chinese Mushrooms and Ginger

Ducks are often seen, comically herded in single file, along the water channels between the rice paddies throughout the country. The substantial Chinese population in Indonesia is particularly fond of duck and the delicious ingredients in this recipe give it an oriental flavour.

INGREDIENTS

Serves 4

2.5kg/5½lb duck
5ml/1 tsp sugar
50ml/2fl oz/¼ cup light soy sauce
2 garlic cloves, crushed
8 dried Chinese mushrooms, soaked in
    350ml/12fl oz/1½ cups warm water
    for 15 minutes
1 onion, sliced
5cm/2in fresh root ginger, sliced and
    cut in matchsticks
200g/7oz baby sweetcorn
½ bunch spring onions, white bulbs left
    whole, green tops sliced
15–30ml/1–2 tbsp cornflour, mixed to
    a paste with 60ml/4 tbsp water
salt and freshly ground black pepper
boiled rice, to serve

1 Cut the duck along the breast, open it up and cut along each side of the backbone. Use the backbone, wings and giblets to make a stock, to use later in the recipe. Any trimmings of fat can be rendered in a frying pan, to use later in the recipe. Cut each leg and each breast in half. Place in a bowl, rub with the sugar and then pour over the soy sauce and garlic.

2 Drain the mushrooms, reserving the soaking liquid. Trim and discard the stalks.

3 Fry the onion and ginger in the duck fat, in a frying pan, until they give off a good aroma. Push to one side. Lift the duck pieces out of the soy sauce and fry them until browned. Add the mushrooms and reserved liquid.

4 Add 600ml/1 pint/2½ cups of the duck stock or water to the browned duck pieces. Season, cover and cook over a gentle heat for about 1 hour, until the duck is tender.

5 Add the sweetcorn and the white part of the spring onions and cook for a further 10 minutes. Remove from the heat and add the cornflour paste. Return to the heat and bring to the boil, stirring. Cook for 1 minute until glossy. Serve, scattered with the spring onion tops, with boiled rice.

VARIATION

Replace the corn with chopped celery and slices of drained, canned water chestnuts.

Aromatic Chicken from Madura

Magadip is best cooked ahead so that the flavours permeate the chicken flesh making it even more delicious. A cool cucumber salad is a good accompaniment.

INGREDIENTS

Serves 4

1.5kg/3–3½lb chicken, cut in quarters, or 4 chicken quarters
5ml/1 tsp sugar
30ml/2 tbsp coriander seeds
10ml/2 tsp cumin seeds
6 whole cloves
2.5ml/½ tsp ground nutmeg
2.5ml/½ tsp ground turmeric
1 small onion
2.5cm/1in fresh root ginger, peeled and sliced
300ml/½ pint/1¼ cups chicken stock or water
salt and freshly ground black pepper
boiled rice and Deep-fried Onions, to serve

1 Cut each chicken quarter in half to obtain eight pieces. Place in a flameproof casserole, sprinkle with sugar and salt and toss together. This helps release the juices in the chicken. Use the backbone and any remaining carcass to make chicken stock for use later in the recipe, if you like.

—— COOK'S TIP ——

Add a large piece of bruised ginger and a small onion to the chicken stock to ensure a good flavour.

2 Dry-fry the coriander, cumin and whole cloves until the spices give off a good aroma. Add the nutmeg and turmeric and heat briefly. Grind in a food processor or a pestle and mortar.

3 If using a processor, process the onion and ginger until finely chopped. Otherwise, finely chop the onion and ginger and pound to a paste with a pestle and mortar. Add the spices and stock or water and mix well.

4 Pour over the chicken in the flameproof casserole. Cover with a lid and cook over a gentle heat until the chicken pieces are really tender, about 45–50 minutes.

5 Serve portions of the chicken, with the sauce, on boiled rice, scattered with crisp Deep-fried Onions.

Balinese Spiced Duck

There is a delightful hotel on the beach at Sanur which cooks this delicious duck dish perfectly.

INGREDIENTS

Serves 4

8 duck portions, fat trimmed
   and reserved
50g/2oz desiccated coconut
175ml/6fl oz/³⁄₄ cup coconut milk
salt and freshly ground black pepper
Deep-fried Onions and salad leaves or
   fresh herb sprigs, to garnish

For the spice paste
1 small onion or 4–6 shallots, sliced
2 garlic cloves, sliced
2.5cm/¹⁄₂ in fresh root ginger, peeled
   and sliced
1cm/¹⁄₂ in fresh *lengkuas*, peeled
   and sliced
2.5cm/1in fresh turmeric or 2.5ml/
   ¹⁄₂ tsp ground turmeric
1–2 red chillies, seeded and sliced
4 macadamia nuts or 8 almonds
5ml/1 tsp coriander seeds, dry-fried

1 Place the duck fat trimmings in a heated frying pan, without oil, and allow the fat to render. Reserve the fat.

2 Dry-fry the desiccated coconut in a preheated pan until crisp and brown in colour.

3 To make the spice paste, blend the onion or shallots, garlic, ginger, *lengkuas*, fresh or ground turmeric, chillies, nuts and coriander seeds to a paste in a food processor or with a pestle and mortar.

4 Spread the spice paste over the duck portions and leave to marinate in a cool place for 3–4 hours. Preheat the oven to 160°C/325°F/ Gas 3. Shake off the spice paste and transfer the duck breasts to an oiled roasting tin. Cover with a double layer of foil and cook the duck in the oven for 2 hours.

5 Turn the oven temperature up to 190°C/375°F/Gas 5. Heat the reserved duck fat in a pan, add the spice paste and fry for 1–2 minutes. Stir in the coconut milk and simmer for 2 minutes. Discard the duck juices then cover the duck with the spice mixture and sprinkle with the toasted coconut. Cook in the oven for 20–30 minutes.

6 Arrange the duck on a warm serving platter and sprinkle with the Deep-fried Onions. Season to taste and serve with the salad leaves or fresh herb sprigs of your choice.

Chicken with Turmeric

INGREDIENTS

Serves 4

1.5kg/3–3½lb chicken, cut in 8 pieces,
    or 4 chicken quarters, each halved
15ml/1 tbsp sugar
3 macadamia nuts or 6 almonds
2 garlic cloves, crushed
1 large onion, quartered
2.5cm/1in fresh *lengkuas*, peeled and
    sliced, or 5ml/1 tsp *lengkuas* powder
1–2 lemon grass stems, lower 5cm/2in
    sliced, top bruised
1cm/½in cube *terasi*
4cm/1½in fresh turmeric, peeled and
    sliced, or 15ml/1 tbsp
    ground turmeric
15ml/1 tbsp tamarind pulp, soaked in
    150ml/¼ pint/⅔ cup warm water
60–90ml/4–6 tbsp oil
400ml/14fl oz/1⅔ cups coconut milk
salt and freshly ground black pepper
Deep-fried Onions, to garnish

1 Rub the chicken joints with a little
  sugar and set them aside.

2 Grind the nuts and garlic in a food
  processor with the onion, *lengkuas*,
sliced lemon grass, *terasi*, and turmeric.
Alternatively, pound the ingredients to
a paste with a pestle and mortar. Strain
the tamarind pulp and reserve the juice.

3 Heat the oil in a wok and cook the
  paste, without browning, until it
gives off a spicy aroma. Add the pieces
of chicken and toss well in the spices.
Add the strained tamarind juice. Spoon
the coconut cream off the top of the
milk and set it to one side.

4 Add the coconut milk to the pan.
  Cover and cook for 45 minutes,
or until the chicken is tender.

5 Just before serving, stir in the
  coconut cream while bringing to
the boil. Season and serve at once,
garnished with Deep-fried Onions.

Balti Baby Chicken in Tamarind Sauce

The tamarind in this recipe gives the dish a sweet and sour flavour; this is also quite a hot Balti.

INGREDIENTS

Serves 4–6

60ml/4 tbsp tomato ketchup
15ml/1 tbsp tamarind paste
60ml/4 tbsp water
7.5ml/1½ tsp chilli powder
7.5ml/1½ tsp salt
15ml/1 tbsp sugar
7.5ml/1½ tsp ginger pulp
7.5ml/1½ tsp garlic pulp
30ml/2 tbsp desiccated coconut
30ml/2 tbsp sesame seeds
5ml/1 tsp poppy seeds
5ml/1 tsp ground cumin
7.5ml/1½ tsp ground coriander
2 x 450g/1lb baby chickens, skinned and cut into 6–8 pieces
75ml/5 tbsp corn oil
120ml/8 tbsp curry leaves
2.5ml/½ tsp onion seeds
3 large dried red chillies
2.5ml/½ tsp fenugreek seeds
10–12 cherry tomatoes
45ml/3 tbsp chopped fresh coriander
2 fresh green chillies, chopped

2 Add the chilli powder, salt, sugar, ginger, garlic, coconut, sesame seeds, poppy seeds, ground cumin and ground coriander to the mixture.

3 Add the chicken pieces to the bowl and stir until they are well coated with the spice mixture. Set aside.

4 Heat the oil in a preheated wok. When it is hot, add the curry leaves, onion seeds, dried red chillies and fenugreek seeds and fry for 1 minute.

5 Lower the heat to medium and add the chicken pieces, together with their sauce, 2 or 3 pieces at a time. When all the chicken has been added to the wok, stir to mix well.

6 Simmer gently for 12–15 minutes or until the chicken is thoroughly cooked through.

7 Add the tomatoes, fresh coriander and green chillies to the wok and serve immediately.

1 Put the tomato ketchup, tamarind paste and water into a large mixing bowl and blend together with a fork.

Soy-braised Chicken

As the chicken is braised in the wok, so the spicy ginger sauce releases its flavour into the meat to create a succulent dish. Enjoy it hot or cold.

INGREDIENTS

Serves 6–8

1 chicken, about 1.5kg/3–3¹⁄₂lb
15ml/1 tbsp ground Szechuan peppercorns
30ml/2 tbsp minced fresh root ginger
45ml/3 tbsp light soy sauce
30ml/2 tbsp dark soy sauce
45ml/3 tbsp Chinese rice wine or dry sherry
15ml/1 tbsp light brown sugar
vegetable oil, for deep-frying
about 600ml/1 pint/2¹⁄₂ cups stock or water
10ml/2 tsp salt
25g/1oz crystal sugar
lettuce leaves, to serve

1 Rub the chicken both inside and out with the ground pepper and fresh ginger. Marinate the chicken with the soy sauces, rice wine or sherry and sugar for at least 3 hours, turning it several times.

— COOK'S TIP —

Any sauce that is left over can be stored, covered, in the refrigerator to be re-used again and again.

2 Heat the oil in a preheated wok, remove the chicken from the marinade and deep-fry for 5–6 minutes, or until brown all over. Remove and drain.

3 Pour off the excess oil, add the marinade with the stock or water, salt and rock sugar and bring to the boil. Cover and braise the chicken in the sauce for 35–40 minutes, turning once or twice.

4 Remove the chicken from the wok and let it cool down a little before chopping it into approximately 30 bitesize pieces. Arrange on a bed of lettuce leaves, then pour some of the sauce over the chicken and serve.

Khara Masala Balti Chicken

Whole spices – *khara* – are used in this recipe, giving it a wonderfully rich flavour. This is a dry dish, so it is best served with raita and paratha.

INGREDIENTS

Serves 4

3 curry leaves
1.5ml/¼ tsp mustard seeds
1.5ml/¼ tsp fennel seeds
1.5ml/¼ tsp onion seeds
2.5ml/½ tsp crushed dried red chillies
2.5ml/½ tsp white cumin seeds
1.5ml/¼ tsp fenugreek seeds
2.5ml/½ tsp crushed pomegranate seeds
5ml/1 tsp salt
5ml/1 tsp shredded ginger
3 garlic cloves, sliced
60ml/4 tbsp corn oil
4 fresh green chillies, slit
1 large onion, sliced
1 medium tomato, sliced
675g/1½lb chicken, skinned, boned and cubed
15 ml/1 tbsp chopped fresh coriander, to garnish
paratha, to serve

2 Add the shredded ginger and garlic cloves to the bowl.

3 Heat the oil in a preheated wok. When the oil is hot, add the spice mixture, then the green chillies.

4 Add the onion to the wok and stir-fry over a medium heat for 5–7 minutes.

5 Add the tomato and chicken pieces to the wok and cook over a medium heat for about 7 minutes or until the chicken is cooked through and the sauce has reduced slightly.

6 Stir the mixture over the heat for a further 3–5 minutes, then garnish with the chopped fresh coriander and serve with the paratha.

1 Mix together the curry leaves, mustard seeds, fennel seeds, onion seeds, crushed red chillies, cumin seeds, fenugreek seeds and crushed pomegranate seeds in a large bowl. Add the salt.

Chicken with Spices and Soy Sauce

A very simple recipe, called *Ayam Kecap,* which will often appear as one of the dishes on a Padang restaurant menu. Any leftovers taste equally good when reheated the following day.

INGREDIENTS

Serves 4

1.5kg/3–3½lb chicken, jointed and cut in 16 pieces
3 onions, sliced
about 1 litre/1¾ pints/4 cups water
3 garlic cloves, crushed
3–4 fresh red chillies, seeded and sliced, or 15ml/1 tbsp chilli powder
45–60ml/3–4 tbsp oil
2.5ml/½ tsp ground nutmeg
6 whole cloves
5ml/1 tsp tamarind pulp, soaked in 45ml/3 tbsp warm water
30–45ml/2–3 tbsp dark or light soy sauce
salt
fresh red chilli shreds, to garnish
boiled rice, to serve

1 Prepare the chicken and place the pieces in a large pan with one of the onions. Pour over enough water to just cover. Bring to the boil and then reduce the heat and simmer gently for 20 minutes.

2 Grind the remaining onions, with the garlic and chillies, to a fine paste in a food processor or with a pestle and mortar. Heat a little of the oil in a wok or frying pan and cook the paste to bring out the flavour, but do not allow to brown.

3 When the chicken has cooked for 20 minutes, lift it out of the stock in the pan using a draining spoon and put it straight into the spicy mixture. Toss everything together over a fairly high heat so that the spices permeate the chicken pieces. Reserve 300ml/½ pint/1¼ cups of the chicken stock to add to the pan later.

4 Stir in the nutmeg and cloves. Strain the tamarind and add the tamarind juice and the soy sauce to the chicken. Cook for a further 2–3 minutes, then add the reserved stock.

5 Taste and adjust the seasoning and cook, uncovered, for a further 25–35 minutes, until the chicken pieces are tender.

6 Serve the chicken in a bowl, topped with shredded chilli, and eat with boiled rice.

COOK'S TIP

Dark soy sauce is thicker and more salty than light. Adding the dark variety will give a deeper colour to the chicken.

Thai Stir-fry Chicken Curry

Here chicken and potatoes are simmered in a wok filled with coconut milk, one of the essential ingredients of Thai cuisine. The end result is a superb flavoursome curry.

INGREDIENTS

Serves 4

1 onion
15ml/1 tbsp groundnut oil
400ml/14fl oz/1²/₃ cups coconut milk
30ml/2 tbsp red curry paste
30ml/2 tbsp Thai fish sauce (*nam pla*)
15ml/1 tbsp soft light brown sugar
225g/8oz tiny new potatoes
450g/1lb skinless chicken breasts,
    cut into chunks
15ml/1 tbsp lime juice
30ml/2 tbsp chopped fresh mint
15ml/1 tbsp chopped fresh basil
salt and ground black pepper
2 kaffir lime leaves, shredded, and 1–2
    fresh red chillies, seeded and finely
    shredded, to garnish

1 Cut the onion into wedges, using a sharp knife.

COOK'S TIP

You can use boneless chicken thighs instead of breasts. Simply skin them, cut the flesh into chunks and cook in the coconut milk with the potatoes.

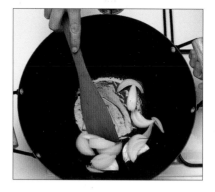

2 Heat a wok until hot, add the oil and swirl it around. Add the onion and stir-fry for 3–4 minutes.

3 Pour in the coconut milk, then bring to the boil, stirring. Stir in the curry paste, fish sauce and sugar.

4 Add the potatoes and seasoning, cover and simmer gently for about 20 minutes.

5 Add the chicken chunks, cover and cook over a low heat for a further 10–15 minutes, until the chicken and potatoes are tender.

6 Stir in the lime juice, chopped mint and basil. Serve at once, sprinkled with the shredded kaffir lime leaves and red chillies.